Are you confused by what the world is saying about woman's role in society? Do you feel you may not be "living up to your potential"? Do you feel you should be a "self-made woman"? Exactly what are you supposed to be doing with your life?

In WOMAN, Dale Evans Rogers takes a close look at the roles women play in the world—both in and out of the home. Using her knowledge of Scripture and her knowledge of life's realities, she maps out a viable, reasonable, biblical path that can lead to true fulfillment for all women. Whether you are a full-time homemaker or work outside the home, God has the answers you need in your life, and WOMAN will help you to understand what they are.

Dale Evans Rogers

with Carole C. Carlson

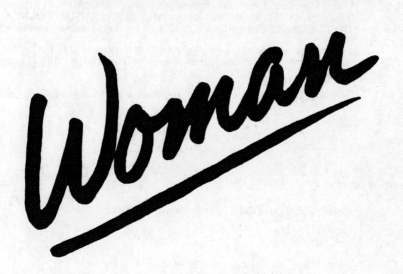

Woman

Power Books

FLEMING H. REVELL COMPANY
OLD TAPPAN, NEW JERSEY

Unless otherwise identified, Scripture quotations in this volume are from the
New American Standard Bible, Copyright © THE LOCKMAN FOUNDA-
TION 1960,1962,1963,1968,1971,1972,1973,1975 and are used by permission.

Scripture quotations identified LB are from The Living Bible, Copyright ©
1971 by Tyndale House Publishers, Wheaton, Illinois 60187. All rights reserved.

Scripture quotations identified KJV are from the King James Version of the
Bible.

Library of Congress Cataloging in Publication Data

Rogers, Dale Evans.
    Woman.

    1. Women—Religious life. 2. Women—Conduct of
life. 3. Rogers, Dale Evans. I. Carlson, Carole C.,
joint author. II. Title.
BV4527.R63   248.8'43   79-27090
ISBN 0-8007-5069-1

Contents

5

Foreword

Someone said to me, "Dale Evans and Roy Rogers are bigger than life." Someone else said, "They're a legend in their own lifetimes." For any human beings that's an impossible image to sustain. Cracks in one's character may appear to be canyons, when they come under public scrutiny.

As I drove through the desert toward the office of this world-renowned woman, I thought, *Why does Dale Evans Rogers want to write a book about women? She'll be open to criticism and misunderstanding. On the other hand, does she really have anything to say that's different?*

And then I met her. Dale *is* different. She doesn't think or act like a celebrity. I've discovered that she races through airports, pulling a little cart piled high with her luggage. She has a small, nonprestige car, which she drives herself on those frequent long trips from her home to the Los Angeles Airport. She avoids the elite salons and designers and has her clothes made by a local dressmaker. She would rather have an omelet in my kitchen than dine in an exclusive restaurant.

Here is a woman who has been plagued by tragedy and triumphed over depression. She drives herself relentlessly not because of fame or fortune—neither of which she needs—but because there is work to be done for others.

Dale's ideas are original and her beliefs gut-level. The only reason she has me tagging along with her on this book is that she needed another woman as a sounding board, and a journalist to help her corral the thoughts that tumble out of her racing mind.

Above all, Dale Evans Rogers is a performing artist. She studies to present the very best for her audience. Mostly, she studies to present herself "approved to God."

Watch out, women; she will surprise, shock, challenge, and inspire you. She may even help you be a better woman. She did me.

CAROLE C. CARLSON

Woman

1
Will the Real Dale Evans Rogers Stand Up?

WOMAN. How many sounds there are in one word! Hear it as a command or a caress. Clothe it in dignity or degrade it with scorn. *Woman*. The identification can be a breeding place for resentment or a source of joy.

Woman, who are you? There's such confusion in the ranks. For years I've thought about the women I've known, the changes which have evolved in the status of our sex, and I've dodged the compulsion to write this book.

Why would I be so hesitant to speak out on the subject? No one has ever accused me of avoiding issues, particularly if they arouse differences in opinions. The reason may be that my convictions and emotions are often in conflict. I have experienced the challenges of being a working woman both inside and outside the home. These careers can be compatible or contrary.

Taking a Stand

Where do I stand? Frankly, it's somewhere between Phyllis Schlafly, Marabel Morgan, Anita Bryant, Betty

13

Friedan, Jane Fonda, and Gloria Steinem. They all have a point. Maybe you're sayin, "Okay, Dale, then why don't you keep quiet, until you know your exact position?" I'll tell you why. Our world is off its spiritual axis, dipping and whirling in a chaos of change. The prevalent twentieth-century mood credits everyone with his own opinion, no matter how rational or irrational that might be. However, the Word of God says, "Come now, and let us reason together . . ." (Isaiah 1:18). All right, let's do just that, with the Holy Bible as our frame of reference.

Why the Bible? I have lived the years of my life both with and without it, as my personal Guidebook. I know from experience that this Best-seller of all times is totally sufficient for "teaching, for reproof, for correction, for training in righteousness" (2 Timothy 3:16). Without the Bible I would have no right to make specific statements about WOMAN.

Many of my views are contrary to prevailing trends. As a woman who has experienced more than sixty years in this earthly pilgrimage, I've seen change, change, change in the status of women. We've come a long way, Baby—but are we really enjoying the trip?

I am an aggressive, creative, sensitive, and vulnerable woman. Whether I call myself *Miss*, *Mrs.*, *Ms.*, or *Madame* makes no difference. I am a female. I know I was created in the image of God, but it doesn't bother me whether I was created first or second in God's order. The point is that, He "saw it was not good for man to be alone" (*see* Genesis 2:18), and He created woman to be man's helper. When the Bible speaks of *man*, it includes *woman*. We are an integral part of *mankind*.

Whether we are male or female, the Bible says God sees us as one, equal, and without prejudice. We are the same in His eyes. He created unique physical beings whom He loves. He is not willing for any of us to die spiritually. However, when He created us He gave us free wills, so that the decision to choose God's way or not is up to us.

I'm laying it on the line in this book. First of all, I'm talking to myself, but if the shoe fits anybody else, then wear it. Many times it will pinch my own toes, but there are some things I must say. I've never been one to keep quiet about what I believe!

There is no animosity in my heart against anyone. God loves each one of us, but He doesn't love everything we do. I can love you, but condemn what you are doing. Look, I'm not flying any self-righteous banner. I've never been perfect and I'm not perfect now. However, I know that the faster I ran from God and His plan for my life—according to the guidelines given to the prophets of old and to Jesus and His disciples—the deeper the quagmire of difficulty I experienced.

Don't Tell Me

I was a rebellious teenager, wanting to have my own way and disobeying my parents. I eloped with a boy who was as emotionally immature as I. I had a baby, but was deprived of raising my son, when I was forced to go to work after his father deserted us. Stinging from that rejection, I developed into what would be termed today a "feminist." I fumed over a woman's lot! I resented a man's being able to do anything *he* wanted and go scot-free, while a woman who might do the same thing was considered a tramp.

My son and I moved in with my mother and I began to work in an office. Soon I began dating, and my mother insisted that I come in at a reasonable hour. She would wait up for me, for I was still in my teens. It made me furious. I thought, *Surely being a mother, I shouldn't be treated as a child myself!*

If my mother spanked Tom, I would churn with resentment. But she loved my son with intense devotion. When he was only two, she probably saved him from what could have been a very dangerous mastoid operation. For two days and nights she stood by him, applying ice packs day and night and unselfishly nursing him.

My gratitude to my mother at that time was shallow. I was much too busy with my own struggles in growing up to appreciate what she was contributing to those important early years in the life of my child. It was the Depression and, like everyone else, I was struggling for economic survival.

When I was in my early twenties, I worked for a large firm and found my office life complicated by one of the bosses. I was constantly dodging his passes; he threatened to have me fired if I complained to the department head about him. I desperately needed that job, so I tolerated his sly remarks and insulting advances as long as I could. Then one day I blew sky high, went to my superior in the firm, and spilled everything. I kept my job and the office playboy kept his, but relations were very strained at work.

I was a young woman who was running in many

ways. Mostly, I was running from the Lord. My life had no direction, I was going in circles. I began to sink deeper into the quicksand of self-seeking, moral turpitude, impulsive decisions, and then complete despair. Guilt feelings began to mount, which led to self-recrimination and feelings of inadequacy. I deceived myself into thinking that I could escape through the ways of the world: alcohol, wrong relationships, pills. Nothing helped. I tried books on psychology, psychiatry, philosophy. But the guilt, which was buried deep within me, was intensified.

As the years passed, my life was filled with trial-and-error experiences. I wrote of those times in my book *The Woman at the Well*.

My Mother, My Son

How I thank God for my Christian mother! She cared enough to teach my son the true way to find himself. Early in his life she taught him by her example and admonition, "In all your ways acknowledge Him, and He will make your paths straight" (Proverbs 3:6). Today he is a success mentally, physically, spiritually, and a credit to his profession as Minister of Music in a large Baptist church near Sacramento.

It was my son Tom who led me to a real commitment of my life to God through Jesus Christ.

In the spring of 1948 I returned to the God of my mother and father. When I came to Him in utter abandon, through the merits and sacrifice of Jesus Christ, His Son, I found His promise of release was true. The Bible says, "As far as the east is from the west, so far has

He removed our transgressions from us" (Psalms 103:12).

Now God's Word is either true or a lie. My burden of guilt was lifted, just as He promised. As the wrong desires in my life began to fade, in their place came desires to please Him. I embarked on a dedicated course of thanking in word and deed my beloved mother. The Lord gave me the years from 1948 until her death in 1976 to show my appreciation to the one who taught me from babyhood that God loved me—that He might not love some of the things I was doing, but He loved me enough to allow His only Son to die for me—that I might have everlasting life by accepting His Wonderful Gift.

As I started to study the Word of God for guidance, my life slowly changed. I began to walk in the brightness of His love, when before I was running in darkness, impulsively turning this way and that, with nothing permanently satisfying me. I don't mean to imply that today, as a Christian, I always bat a thousand. I still goof. However, He has quickened my spirit and my conscience, and the red danger light starts flashing within me, when I'm off base. The Lord is faithful and ever ready to hear my plea for forgiveness and help.

There is a line in the classic *Hound of Heaven* by Francis Thompson: "All things betray thee, who betrayest Me." What a truth! The lures of the world, devious humanistic plans never satisfy the deepest longings of the soul. Saint Augustine said:

Thou has made us for Thyself, and the heart of man is restless until it finds its rest in Thee.

I raced for years, trying to find happiness. It eluded me. There were so many things I wanted, but when I got some of them, I wasn't satisfied. The Bible says, "Delight yourself in the Lord; and He will give you the desires of your heart" (Psalms 37:4). If I had delighted myself in His Word and in fellowship with Him and other Christians in my youth, He would have given me the right desires for those things which would glorify Him and ultimately give the greatest happiness.

I believe happiness is a sense of fulfillment. We have it when we know we are accomplishing what we are meant to do. What are we to do in this great world of ours? Certainly we were born for a purpose.

2
Here I Am—
Where Are You?

My friend Carole, who is working with me on this book, read the first rough draft and said, "Dale, you write in a very earthy way. People will relate to what you're saying, because they can identify with you." I guess I am an earthy person, because I know I'm earthbound during this life. But, believe me, I am filled with a soaring spirit. That's God's grace, not my own wings flapping in the breeze.

I make no apologies for my lack of academic journalism. My desire is to communicate to men, women, and children on a one-to-one basis concerning their relationship with God through Jesus Christ. I have no intention to pussyfoot on delicate issues, nor to soothe ears that "go around looking for teachers who will tell them just what they want to hear" (2 Timothy 4:3 LB). I know the stark personal reality of this description: "They won't listen to what the Bible says but will blithely follow their own misguided ideas" (v. 4).

God has given me the courage to face up to myself, and sometimes this isn't a particularly joyous discovery.

Whenever I reach a point at which I begin to wonder who I am and whether what I'm doing is worth it, the Lord seems to answer my unexpressed questions.

One morning when Roy was out of town I attended church via television. My hungry soul was fed abundantly, as I listened to Chuck Smith of Calvary Chapel, Costa Mesa, California, say, "We hear much talk about 'finding ourselves,' who we are . . . and all of the other nebulous phrases we apply in our search for personal identity. . . ." Then he looked straight into the eye of the camera and stated this strong truth: "Instead of worrying about who we are and finding ourselves, we must first find God." He explained that when we find Him we will find our true selves in Him. Wow! I was all alone in the house, with only the animals to hear me. I shouted, "Hallelujah!"

By God's grace, I endeavor to explain to the folks the essential and eternal meaning of "finding yourself" every time I witness or do a gospel concert.

Beyond the Looking Glass

To "find yourself" on a strictly humanistic basis is almost always a disappointing experience. Women are getting caught up in so many pursuits today that lead to dead ends on a street going nowhere. I was listening to a radio-talk show the other night when the interviewer, a woman who openly admitted she was "agnostic," was questioning her guests about their involvement with "Krishna Consciousness." Before the interview was over the talk-show hostess admitted that she was searching for a "deeper meaning in her life," and thought that a "religious experience" via the application of the meditative processes of Krishna Consciousness could be the answer to her need.

Oh, my, how I wish I could have been on that program! I know "experiences" are not the answer to meaning in life. Many women are trying to make a career or a job fill the gap in their personal identity crises. Others cram their lives with social or community projects, or concentrate on physical fitness. We try this and that, bouncing from one activity to another, discarding this avenue because it has flaws, and looking for another path.

The relentless need to *be* somebody bogs down when nothing seems to satisfy. The truth of the matter is, in my humble opinion, that we are unable to change the inherent weakness in our natures because of original sin in our flesh. Hey, don't tune me out yet, if you happen to be one who scoffs at original sin. I don't believe the Bible teaches that we come into this life all good and pure, and then the world pollutes us. Because Eve yielded to the temptation of Satan and ate the forbidden fruit, fellowship was broken with Almighty God, and that nasty little three letter word *sin* became man's plight. I'm so happy God loved us so much that He provided a way for our sins to be forgiven.

If God didn't care about us, He would have left us to flap around like a bird with its wings clipped. We'd never get off the ground. He could have said, "You folks down there are so smart, you'll just have to find your own way to take care of your sin and guilt."

Without God our efforts to find ourselves are so puny.

Identity Through Marriage

For some women, the search to find themselves narrows to the hunt for a husband. When a woman believes she must be a Mrs. to be complete as an individual, she may settle for less than God's best for her life.

Recently I heard about the tragic results of a Christian woman who married an atheist. She had a daughter who was dominated and influenced by her atheistic father. The girl was in her midteens, when she committed suicide. What happened to confuse this poor child so much that she would take her life? Perhaps she tried to meet her mother's ideals through the humanistic efforts taught by her father and couldn't cut it, so she "cut out" in desperation.

I wish all young women would listen to the words of the late, beloved spiritual giantess, Henrietta Mears. She said, "Be careful whom you date; you might just wind up marrying him!" She was referring to the Christian becoming unequally yoked with an unbeliever.

Almighty God put a spiritual searchlight in us women, and He intends for us to use it to find Him. Saint Paul said, "Follow me, as I follow Christ" (*see* 1 Corinthians 11:1). If we find ourselves in a conversion, born-again experience in Jesus Christ and we are married to unbelievers, our allegiance, according to my understanding, is first to God. We are to obey our husbands in the Lord. If he disparages our faith, we must stand firm in Jesus, not allowing anything or anybody to draw us from our beliefs. Jesus said that in heaven there is no marrying, nor giving in marriage, but we are as angels (Matthew 22:30). We must never lose sight of this truth. Loving our husbands to the exclusion of loving Christ is never the ultimate answer to our emptiness, even though a good marriage seems to be completely fulfilling.

In the first and last analysis, our allegiance is to God, through Jesus Christ.

The Great Image Maker

Women, all this furore about "doing your own thing," "finding out who you are," *ad infinitum* into the introspective probing, can be resolved by discovering a right relationship with God in Jesus Christ. The Bible says of the Son of God:

> He is the image of the invisible God, the firstborn of all creation. For in Him all things were created, both in the heavens and on earth, visible and invisible, whether thrones or dominions or rulers or authorities—all things have been created through Him and for Him. And He is before all things, and in Him all things hold together.
>
> Colossians 1:15-17

I know that I could not "hold together," except through the power of Jesus Christ. Think of it. He knows exactly what went into our creation. He gave each one of us gifts to use. There isn't one thing about us women that He doesn't know. Isn't it about time we realize He knows best how to use what He created? He not only gave us the directions for our lives, He wrote the copy. Let us submit ourselves totally to Him who can make our lives count to the fullest of our potential.

Appearance is so important to many people. We worry about the length of our noses or the color of our hair; we fret about our looks and wish we looked like someone else. And yet God created us, He assembled our features and our bodies in some particular sequence. What makes the difference in our appearance is the way *He* works within us.

Roy and I were on the "Merv Griffin Show" one night when Merv said, "What is it about you Christians that gives you a certain shine?" In my humble opinion, that was the greatest accolade ever given us. If there's any shine to be seen, it's the Spirit of Jesus, not of ourselves. We are simply earthen vessels offered for His use; we are faulty and vulnerable. The brightness of any shine depends on our willingness to turn up our wick of availability for greater spiritual flame in our lives.

To sincerely embark on a true Christian pilgrimage is to lay your life on the line for Jesus, not counting the cost, but looking toward the ultimate joy in being molded and fitted for eternity with Him.

We are, according to God's Word, bought with a price (1 Corinthians 6:20). We do not belong to ourselves. To declare, "I will be the master of my fate" is to be blinded by the arch deceiver, Satan. Remember, it was he who tempted Eve with "Eat the forbidden fruit and you will be like God" (*see* Genesis 3:5). Frankly, women, I want my God to be a very big God, larger than I could ever possibly become in this flesh.

There's Something About That Name

In my years in show business I've found that one name can produce an immediate embarrassed hush in the midst of a conversation. When Jesus Christ is mentioned respectfully and reverently, there may be a strain in the atmosphere. Speak of Him in a blasphemous manner, and there is little reaction. It is incredible to me that society can talk of anything or anybody, from presidents, prime ministers, athletic figures, movie stars, UFOs—anything—except the Lord Jesus Christ.

I am probably striking a nerve in some, but as my Grandmother Smith said, "Facts are facts." Just why is the name of *Jesus Christ* cause for discomfort? Without a doubt, He stands above every man and woman throughout history. Even our calendar is based on His advent into human history. To speak boldly of one's faith in God and His Christ, in the world's opinion, is to invite criticism and often persecution.

I was to do a television commercial one time and was wearing a little cross around my neck. This was very precious to me, because I had bought it with a small inheritance my father left me when he died. I was told I couldn't wear it on TV because it might offend some people. I refused to take it off, alienating the producer.

"Religion is personal, private, and no one should foist his beliefs on anyone else," he said.

I've heard this, or variations on this theme, many times in my life. If you are a believer in Jesus Christ, as the Messiah, how can you remain quiet about it? Didn't He command His followers, "And this gospel of the kingdom shall be preached in the whole world for a

witness to all nations, and then the end shall come"
(Matthew 24:14).

Instead of so much worrisome conjecture over UFOs
signaling the end of time, we should be attending to our
charge of being witnesses to the reality of salvation in
Jesus Christ. He commanded us to "Occupy till I come"
(Luke 19:13 KJV). That's to keep busy with His work!
Someday He will split the heavens and come for those
who believe in Him. This event has been called the
"Rapture" by believers. Personally, the theological ar-
guments about when this will take place don't matter to
me. What does matter is that I am ready, with ample oil
of the Holy Spirit in my lamp when the Bridegroom
comes for His bride, the church, or body of believers.
He demands that we *do* as well as believe. He said,
"Follow Me," and that doesn't mean to sit on a rock
and wait for Him to come again. He also cautioned that
not all who would call Him "Lord, Lord" would be in
His Kingdom, but "he that doeth the will of my Father:"
(Matthew 7:21 KJV). A very fine preacher, Royal Blue of
Redding, California, says, "Christians should 'walk the
talk.' " Amen, and amen . . . and both *amens* are for
you, Dale, do you hear?

The Searching Woman

Last night I was rereading Anne Morrow Lindbergh's
priceless *Gift From the Sea*. I read it years ago, but today I
am basking in the beauty, sensitivity, and honesty of
that woman's bared soul. This book is a real gem of one
woman's seeking for inward strength, for arrangement
of priorities. She said, "Woman today is still searching.

We are aware of our hunger and needs, but still ignorant of what will satisfy them."

Here is a woman who suffered the brutal kidnapping and death of her beautiful baby son, and yet the experience did not destroy her. It acted as a powerful refiner of the gold of her soul. In her book she speaks the unspoken longings of most of us women. Mind you, in 1955 this woman was asking the same questions women are asking today. Her pressures were tremendous, and she struggled to be free—at least periodically—to "find herself," to let go of all the demands of worldly trapping. She realized the necessity to discover herself, even to the point of escaping to her beloved shack by the sea, sans modern conveniences. She had a world-famous husband, five children, and a writing career. At times she was so fragmented that the only way she could just be Anne was to shed her pressured life for a period of time.

In her beach hideaway, crude as it was, Anne Lindbergh was able to see her life in true perspective. Listen to one of her revealing statements about her inner longings: "I would like to achieve a state of inner spiritual grace from which I could function and give as I was meant to in the eye of God."

Anne Morrow Lindbergh said, "One must lose one's life to find it." Jesus Christ said, "For whoever wishes to save his life shall lose it; but whoever loses his life for My sake shall find it" (Matthew 16:25).

We cannot all escape to a remote beach shack; however, we can find some nook or cranny, or clean out a closet for our hideaway. Jesus said, "Come away by yourselves to a lonely place and rest a while . . ." (Mark

6:31). He, who was the Son of the Most High, found it necessary to escape from the pressures of the world. Certainly if *He* had to remove Himself from the crowd at times, we need to do the same.

But I'm Busy Now!

I know some women who make a fetish of being busy. Their daily activities are done on the run, panting all the way. I see nothing wrong with hard work and creative activity, but we need to be renewed. Sometimes even fifteen minutes of prayerful meditation, supplication, and thanks will work wonders in a harassed wife, mother, or career woman. We require that hiding place for the restoration of our souls.

There are some crucial decisions for a woman in today's world. The framework of our times is vastly different from the days of Jesus, or even the era of a generation or so ago. However, the underlying needs of woman are the same.

Today woman is caught in the whirlwind of expanding technology, devious political schemes, and unbelievable economic pressures. We hear from every source the insistent questioning of time-honored and -tested spiritual values. While we are struggling in this modern current of confusion, we still long for those basic needs of woman: to love; to be loved; to mother; to make a good home; to contribute God-given talents to community, state, nation, and the world at large. Are these needs too big to be fulfilled?

I submit that these demands cannot be met with any degree of success without God through Jesus Christ.

Without Him at the helm of life, sooner or later even the most efficient, enthusiastic of women will start to crack, either physically or emotionally, or both.

Women, it's just too hard for us to be everything to everybody, all by ourselves. The self-made woman is on the way to self-destruction.

But is anything too hard for God? The Bible says, "With men [and that means women, too] this is impossible, but with God all things are possible" (Matthew 19:26).

Either He is God, or He is not. I believe with all my heart God is real and I have cast my lot with Him. This is where I am. How about you?

3
Who's Responsible?

Women, let's look at the Bible in earnest and see what God has to say about our responsibility. Take a look at the Old and New Testaments. Women have figured prominently on the side of God. They have been a credit to womanhood and have discharged their womanly duties and privileges admirably. The Lord has favored woman time and time again.

A Gentle Woman

It was a woman who bore our Savior. Among all the women in the world, no female has been so honored as Mary, the mother of Jesus. More little girls have been named after her; more variations of her name have been invented than any other female name. God chose a little village girl to be the mother of the King. We don't know anything about her appearance, or her background, but we do know that she was poor. However, throughout the ages, madonnas of the most exquisite beauty have been fashioned to represent Mary.

Among all of the little Jewish girls who believed in Jehovah, God of Israel, why did God choose this humble peasant to be the mother of His only Son? Although this is as mysterious to us as the virgin birth, we know that God in His wisdom chose the perfect mother for the divine Child.

As we learn about the complete willingness of Mary to yield herself to the Lord, we realize the example that God has given us in her. Mary was humble, and yet exalted above all women. Mary was obedient to God, and yet suffered the agony of seeing her Son die. Mary, patient and trusting, submissive and strong, is a gentle reminder of God's great portrait of womanhood.

A Discerning Woman

It was a woman who bore John the Baptist, forerunner of Christ. Elizabeth was a woman with very strong spiritual faith, but a woman who lived for years with a sorrowful heart. She prayed and longed for a child, but was barren. When she and her husband were past the age when the birth of a child seemed possible, an angel appeared and informed them that they were to have a son and should name him John. One of the most amazing stories of spiritual discernment is the account of Elizabeth and the child she carried in her womb. When she was six months pregnant. Elizabeth had a visit from her cousin Mary. As soon as Mary entered her home, the baby ". . . leaped in my womb for joy" (Luke 1:44). Elizabeth was filled with the Holy Spirit and knew that the mother of her long-awaited Messiah was in her presence.

Elizabeth, a woman gifted with spiritual perception, inspires me to trust God when the circumstances appear impossible.

A Patient Woman

It was a woman, Anna the prophetess, who recognized the Infant Jesus as the Messiah (Luke 2:36-38). Anna was one of God's favored women. She was married only seven years before she became a widow, and for eighty-four more years she served the Temple, a devout worshiper and prayer warrior. Anna knew the Old Testament prophecies about the coming Messiah and believed that He would come. When Mary and Joseph brought the little eight-day-old boy to the Temple, as the Law of Moses required, Anna knew this was the Promised One, her long-awaited Savior. Immediately she became a missionary in her own hometown, and ". . . continued to speak of Him to all those who were looking for the redemption of Jerusalem" (Luke 2:38).

Dear, loyal Anna. How many precious women we have in our churches who are faithful in their attendance and prayers! Week after week they pray for the needs of the pastor and the congregation. How reassuring and comforting it must be for the minister to look from his pulpit and see those devout women in loyal attendance.

Anna teaches me the patience of age and the rewards for that patience. She waited for her Messiah and lived to see Him. Perhaps I shall live to see the Second Coming of Christ. Who knows?

A Willing Woman

It was a woman at the well in Samaria to whom Jesus declared Himself the Messiah. What type of woman would be privileged to hear from Jesus Himself the secret of His divinity? His disciples were shocked with the conduct of their Master. Didn't He know who she was? First of all, she was a Samaritan, and Jews had no dealings with these people. They were socially and racially unacceptable. Furthermore, she was *the* woman of Samaria, not just any one. She was well known by the men of the town because of her multiple marriages (if they were, indeed, legal marriages), and for the fact that the man she was living with at that time was not her husband.

When Jesus asked her for a drink of water from the well she was astounded. Then when He told her all about her past and present life, she knew she was in the presence of a prophet. He told her He would give her living water, that she would never thirst again, but have a ". . . well of water springing up to eternal life" (John 4:14). At first what He said was puzzling to her. She knew that He was a prophet, but she was confused about the place she should worship, since both the Jews and the Samaritans had specific places of worship. Jesus taught her that the spirit of worship was more important than the place. Translated into our jargon, that means it doesn't make any difference what church building you attend, or what country you live in, as long as the Spirit of the living God, Jesus Christ, is present in your life.

The unnamed Samaritan woman at the well immediately became an evangelist, hurrying back to her city to tell everyone she had met the Christ for whom both the Samaritans and the Jews had been looking.

The woman at the well is a constant reminder to me

that Jesus Christ is no respecter of your past or your place of birth. There is no racial prejudice, no denominational snobbery, in the teachings of Jesus.

A Forgiven Woman

It was a woman caught in the act of adultery to whom Jesus showed God's impartiality. She was brought before Him by her accusers, who were ready to stone her, according to the Law of Moses. She was undoubtedly guilty of adultery, but why, I ask you, if any stoning was to be done, didn't the Pharisees include the man, who was also an offender? There have to be two to commit adultery! Double standard, you say? What did Jesus say? ". . . He who is without sin among you, let him be the first to throw a stone at her" (John 8:7). All of the accusers left, slinking out one by one. Not one of those men was innocent of the sin of adultery.

The adulterous woman addressed Jesus as *Lord*, a word which indicated her reverence for Him, and the knowledge that He was the only one who had the right to forgive her and cleanse her of her sin. Although we are never told the precise ending to this story, I believe that she went on to lead a life of purity. When she acknowledged Jesus as Lord, His pardon was sufficient to change her life-style and make her become a new person—to be born again.

A Grieving Woman

It was a woman, the widow of Nain, who first experienced the miracle of Christ's power to raise the dead. Throughout the Bible we see the very special and tender

care God has for women who have known the ache and
emptiness of widowhood. When Jesus saw the sad little
funeral procession, He learned of the plight of the griev-
ing woman. Her only son had died, her mainstay and
source of support. The future certainly must have
looked bleak. Jesus had great compassion for her and
against all the customs of the time, because rabbis
feared pollution from the corpse, He touched the dead
boy and commanded, ". . . Young man, I say to you,
arise!" (Luke 7:14). Can you imagine the reaction of the
band of mourners? Jesus was known as a teacher, a
rabbi, but now they saw with their own eyes His first
resurrection miracle. The word spread fast throughout
Galilee.

It was to a woman that Jesus made the wondrous
declaration, "I am the resurrection, and the life; he who
believes in Me shall live even if he dies" (John 11:25).
What a promise! Martha, whose brother, Lazarus, had
just died, had said to Jesus, "Lord, if You had been
here, my brother would not have died" (v. 21). Lazarus
did not remain in the grave, because Jesus performed
another miracle and raised him from the dead. However, to me the greater miracle is that each one who
believes in Jesus Christ and calls Him "Lord," as Martha
did, will live forever. I really don't understand this, because eternity is more than my mind can grasp, but I
believe in Jesus and I trust Him to reveal to me in time
what eternity means.

A Devoted Woman

It was a woman to whom Jesus Christ appeared in His
resurrection body: Mary Magdalene, the tormented

woman whom Jesus cured of what must have been demonic possession. She must have suffered with mental illness for years, before Jesus healed her and restored her sanity. Mary Magdalene became one of the most devoted women disciples, following Jesus to the very foot of the Cross.

Mary Magdalene was present at the trial in Pilate's hall, when the so-called religious leaders of the time shouted for the crucifixion of her Master. She watched with a broken heart the agonies of Christ on the Cross. As the song says, she was there when they crucified her Lord. She was last at the Cross and first at the garden tomb. She witnessed the most important event in world history, and the event upon which Christianity is based: the Resurrection of Jesus Christ. The disciples came and saw that the stone had been rolled away, peeked in, and then do you know what they did? They went home! But not Mary Magdalene. She stood outside the tomb and cried, and as she wept, two angels appeared to her and asked her most tenderly, "Woman, why are you weeping?" Oh, the heartbreak, the pathos in this woman when she replied, "Because they have taken away my Lord, and I do not know where they have laid Him" (John 20:13).

God has given women the depth of compassion to weep for those we love. But He rewards us beyond our understanding, when He calls us by name, as He did this woman. "Woman, why are you weeping?" Then when she heard the voice she knew so well say her name *Mary*, she answered Him instantly with "Rabboni!" which means "Teacher," the strongest expression of love and respect.

Oh, what Christ can do for a woman! He is able to take our tormented souls and give us peace. Mary Magdalene reminds me that once He heals us, there are so many ways we can serve Him, but the most important of all is witnessing to others of His resurrection power.

What a company of women ministered to Jesus! Women, we are responsible to Him today. He desires to use us as He will to bring others into His Kingdom. To fail Him is to fail ourselves and the coming generations. Let us be awake and alert to do His bidding!

Those women who resent being women should read what the Bible says: "Can the thing formed reply to the One who formed it?" (*see* Romans 9:20). Let's not buck it, girls; let's learn what He really means for a woman to be. He has given each one of us fantastic abilities and characteristics, which men do not have!

4
Center Stage

Recognition. Oh, how we long for it! To see your name in print, to hear the applause . . . how sweet. Secretly we say, "Please don't make me a number in a computer. I want to *be* somebody." We love to have someone say, "Hey, you did a good job," or just give us a pat on the back (in public, if possible). But somewhere we know there's a line to be drawn between the need for honest appreciation and ego.

For many years I battled for recognition as an entertainer. I fought for money, billing, and applause. I winced when the ovations for others eclipsed mine. I struggled, as the woman behind the man, wanting more of the glory myself. If I had been a self-effacing, reserved person, this might not have been a problem, but as an outspoken, aggressive female, I found it hard to let a man take credit for anything I thought belonged to me. Resentment builds, when we believe we have not been recognized for our accomplishments.

How I struggled with this battle of ego! I seemed incapable of fighting it. I know some performers who virtually plug their ears to the praise of others because of their own personal insecurity. I was almost that bad before I accepted Jesus as my Savior.

There are some people who don't seem to have that driving need to be center stage. I once knew a man who composed beautiful music. He was a real genius in his field. He was content to hear his compositions played by a large orchestra, but refused to take bows for his own musical talent. I have never forgotten the example he gave me, and I respect him for his lack of concern for public adulation.

It was the power of Jesus Christ in my life that reduced the pressure of competition. He has been teaching me for over thirty years that the joy of performing through His grace is sufficient, not the acclaim I get for it.

The Star Complex

You may say, "But if you hadn't developed your career in show business you wouldn't have gained the ear of so many people. Why are you putting it down?"

I'm certainly not putting down show business. I love it, and I know that what has happened to me has been for a reason. Romans 8:28 (KJV) says, "All things work together for good to them that love God, to them who are the called according to His purpose." My career has worked for good, but in the beginning my intense preoccupation with becoming a success hurt quite a few people.

I hitched my wagon to the star of personal success, based on ego. This may lead to some bad scenes. There were so many things that I wanted and struggled to attain under my own steam. When I finally released some of those desires to God and said, "Okay, if You want it for me, God, then it's fine; if You don't want it, that's fine, too." *Then* some of the very things I desired were given to me.

When we are able to submit ourselves to God and ask Him through Christ to use us, our priorities start to fall in place. We begin to listen to the leading of His Holy Spirit, instead of our egocentric wishes.

Now I see any fame that I have achieved from a new perspective. The awards can be used to glorify God, not for my personal gratification. They are instruments to be used for His goals, not mine. Do you see the difference?

There is a subtle danger in so-called "Christian personalities or celebrities." If they are not thoroughly committed to Jesus and willing to wait upon His Spirit to speak—and act through them—they may get carried away in the flesh and "perform." I understand this dilemma, because I have been in the entertainment business for many years and know how treacherous the ego can be, particularly when there is a large crowd in attendance. It is not the Gospel according to Pat Boone, Norma Zimmer, Nicky Cruz, Chuck Colson, Johnny Cash, Evie, or Roy and Dale Rogers that gets the job done. It's "What is the Gospel according to Jesus Christ?"

Paul said, "Follow me as I follow Christ." He knew the ease with which people can slip into being personality followers. We have seen in our time how strong leaders of cults can entice the weak and gullible into their snares.

Even the most committed Christians are prone to fall short of the glory of God. We are still human. Please,

please do not be a "Christian-celebrity watcher," but a
Christ watcher! We can accomplish this through prayer
and the reading of His Word. We can understand His
life as contained in the Word.

As a Christian witness, I pray the Lord will jerk the
leash on me if I run ahead in the flesh. Believe me, it is
easy to do.

Look At Me, Me, Me

There are people in organizations—both religious and
secular—who I believe actually retard their growth and
accomplishment, because they feel they are not ap-
preciated or recognized for their efforts.

Long ago, in my childhood, I remember a small incident in my mother's family, which troubled me at the
time. My grandfather was presented with a beautiful
cake by Annie, one of his daughters, who was particularly gifted and educated in culinary arts. On the other
hand, another daughter, Hallie, was very talented and
skilled in many ways. The family believed that grandfather praised her more than his other children.

The cake was left in the kitchen, with no note. When
he returned from some errands, he found the luscious
cake on the counter and exclaimed in front of his other
daughters, "Now isn't that just like Hallie!" The sisters
resentfully declared, "Annie Merle baked that cake for
you, Papa."

My Aunt Annie Merle received his thanks, and I
doubt that she ever knew about the incident. It was a
mistaken assumption on his part. He would have been
humiliated if he had known there was any suspicion of

partiality toward his children; he was the fairest man I have ever known. He personally didn't seek recognition for his good deeds; as a matter of fact, he demanded that his acts of financial generosity be kept a secret. When he died, the recipients of his kindness and charity came forward at his funeral and told how he had helped them.

It seems like such a small illustration, but many times those little lessons from our childhood remain with us all our lives. To be overlooked for a personal accomplishment can be crushing. But is it the spirit which is injured or the ego?

When I was in midteens I wrote a song. It was the first creative piece of music I had done, and I was proud of it. However, I was naive about copyrights, and my music was left in a publisher's office, with the thought that they might publish it. Months later I was in a variety store, and there on a sheet-music stand was my song with minor changes. It certainly wasn't my name as composer! I was furious inside over the unfairness.

One of the Commandments is "Thou shalt not covet. . . ." Usually we think of this as wanting something that belongs to someone else, but it's more. It's looking with envy and longing at that new car your brother is driving, or seeing your best friend in an outfit that must have cost a fortune. We may envy someone's husband, children, job, figure, or personality. We wonder why everyone seems to have it better than we do.

Covetousness is more than envy or desire for material things that belong to others. It can mean the desire for praise that goes to someone else, when you did the work. The Lord will reward in His own time and way.

In the long run, the real satisfaction is in the creating
and seeing the finished work. Praise can puff up one's
ego, unless one's life is hidden with Christ in God.
When complimented, if a Christian can say "Praise the
Lord!" and mean it, then the Christian's humility is not
threatened.

The Bible says, "But HE WHO BOASTS, LET HIM BOAST IN
THE LORD. For not he who commends himself is approved, but whom the Lord commends" (2 Corinthians
10:17,18).

I don't think we can afford to relax our vigilance on
buildup of ego. Satan is right there with his sly, "You
know you did the work; why don't you speak up?"
Anytime I have been caught off guard in such an instance and have impulsively spoken up for myself, I
have lost one to Satan. Instantly I am disquieted, because the peace of the Lord has left me.

The Nameless Ones

In the Bible are stories of women who have performed acts which never gave them gold stars on their
charts or pins to wear on their blouses for meritorious
services. In fact some of these women are nameless,
which is the ultimate in nonrecognition.

I think about the little maid of Naaman's wife. How
much lower can you get on the totem pole than being a
Jewish female slave in Syria without a name? And yet,
without any self-seeking motive, she was influential in
the life of a very prominent man, Naaman, the captain
of the Syrian army.

This little Hebrew girl was taken captive in Israel and

brought across the border into Syria to serve Naaman's wife. The little slave became a devoted servant, but knew that her mistress was deeply troubled. She discovered that Naaman, the great warrior, was infected with dreaded leprosy. The incurable disease was taking its toll on the mind and body of her master.

It must have been bold of the maid to offer advice, but she told her mistress of the prophet in Samaria who could cure leprosy. Naaman went to his boss, the king, and received a leave of absence to go to Israel and see this prophet, Elisha. Miracles happened. Naaman was cured of leprosy, but even better, his soul was cleansed. He became a believer in the Lord God Jehovah of Israel.

The maid of Naaman's wife was responsible for her master finding faith in God. Certainly the effect of his conversion must have been felt throughout the kingdom. What about the slave? She was a woman behind the scenes who never received credit.

But I Must Be Assertive

We are being told today that we must have assertiveness training. Look out for number one—push yourself forward—claim your place in the sun! The world is telling us that the only way to be recognized is by putting ourselves in a place of importance.

There is a story in the Bible about a dinner party which could have made the society pages of the *Israel News*. It was held in the home of a prominent Pharisee, who invited all the "best people" in town, and for amusement added a rabble-rouser by the name of Jesus to the guest list. It must have been an unusual party, with the community leaders eyeing this strange rabbi very closely. He was contradicting their rules and threatening their very life-style with His teaching.

Can't you just see it? There was Jesus, standing in the background and watching the invited guests maneuvering for positions at the banquet table. Each one wanted to make sure he had a good seat. (The best tables are in the front, you know.)

Jesus began to speak in a parable to the invited guests and said, "When you are invited by someone to a wedding feast, do not take the place of honor, lest someone more distinguished than you may have been invited by him, and he who invited you both shall come and say to you, 'Give place to this man,' and then in disgrace you proceed to occupy the last place" (Luke 14: 8,9).

How embarrassing! Have you ever pushed in some place only to be told, "Sorry, that's reserved." Jesus continued with His parable by telling them that when they are invited, they should go to the last place. If you do this, when the host comes he will say to you, "Here, take this place over here. I want you to have a better seat." Then you can take the seat of honor.

Jesus said, "For everyone who exalts himself shall be humbled, and he who humbles himself shall be exalted" (v. 11).

I believe that means that when Christ Himself sees our merit, He will reward us, and that no amount of manipulating for recognition is going to mean a thing.

Smooth Ride in the Backseat

I have been learning the lessons of recognition for the last thirty-two years and find that God's rewards are

always the highest. This is, of course, diametrically op-
posed to the world system, but it leads to lasting inner
peace.

Since I am a strictly "up-front" person in my thinking
and actions, humility is hard for me. My background in
show business rates this quality quite low on the scale.
In this profession, performance is based on ego, selling
one's personality, and relying on the words of the critics
for evaluation. One is either up or down, according to
the box-office receipts, media ratings, or public opinion.
This is one of the major reasons that the entertainment
business is a hard row for the Christian to hoe and keep
his eyes on the Lord.

I would rather fall flat on my face for the Lord than
rate star billing.

And He has said to me, "My grace is sufficient
for you, for power is perfected in weakness."
Most gladly, therefore, I will rather boast about
my weaknesses, that the power of Christ may
dwell in me. Therefore I am well content with
weaknesses, with insults, with distresses, with
persecutions, with difficulties, for Christ's sake;
for when I am weak, then I am strong.

2 Corinthians 12:9,10

5
What's My Role?

What's all this fuss about "persons"? We must address a *chairperson* or call for a *fireperson*. In the classified advertisements in many newspapers we can't designate sexual preference. I can't understand some of the issues that are being raised today in regard to the roles of men and women. If the implications of this trend weren't so serious, it would be comical.

Did God create "personkind"?

Let's begin with America. Our country has always been described as female. Certainly we can't deny that the Statue of Liberty is a woman! However, our ancestors are referred to as forefathers and the men who established this republic were the Founding Fathers. There has always been a role for women and a role for men.

Women can't afford to put men down, nor can men put women down. We are meant to complement each other. We need each other! Both men and women are off the beam saying, "I top you; I have no need of you!"

Two by Two

When God created us He gave us special gifts, tremendous potential, which most of us scarcely tap. He also created pairs of both animals and humans for procreation. Noah took pairs on the ark to preserve the promise for the coming generations.

God meant for us to reproduce. If He didn't want the human race to multiply, why did He make males and females?

It baffles me why some women are balking at bearing children. It is even more puzzling why women want to be masculine, and men desire feminine characteristics. What is the basis of this trend toward gender change? I know there are some men and women who may have a hormone imbalance, but is there a possibility that this can be corrected medically? The medical profession has discovered how to perform a complete sex change, except for the ability to bear children. Certainly there must be positive steps which can be taken to help people with sexual variances.

I believe there are some underlying reasons men and women have for sex reversal. Whenever we shake our fists at God and say, "Who needs You?" we are rebelling against our Father's plan for our lives. Rebellion may become a fierce master, which propels us into erratic behavior. This may be the reason there are so many suicides among sexual deviates.

In the entertainment field I have known and loved many people who are controlled by homosexuality. They are, in most cases, talented, charming, helpful, and understanding. However, they are out of God's plan. For those who may say, "Well, that doesn't apply to *me*," there is no reason to feel smug. In the Bible the print of the Law is the same size and density. These traits are also off base spiritually: greed, dishonesty, adultery, malice, gossip, envy . . . you name it. When we fall into these patterns, all types of aberations surface in our lives.

Woman, Be a Woman

I was watching the Mike Douglas talk show one day and heard some comments that hit to the core of the behavior and attitudes of some women today. A very personable Burt Reynolds-type fellow was being interviewed by Douglas. He told Douglas of a recent encounter he had with a woman, after he had appeared on another television program. The woman was resplendent with blond hair, full-length mink coat, and diamond earrings—obviously not a welfare case. Boldly, she asked the young man, "Do you play tennis?" He was surprised by such a question in the halls of the studio, but replied, "Yes, I do, but right now I don't have the equipment to play." Appraising him through her long eyelashes, she drawled, "That's all right; I have all the equipment you need!"

From the way the man told the story, the manner of the woman was brash, with double meaning. He said he was reduced to sputtering.

Mike Douglas listened to the story and commented that women amaze him today. He continued that he finds himself unable to answer adequately some of their boldness and audacity. "They aren't acting like women anymore!" He was incredulous. "Why, women are saying and doing the things men used to do, and I don't know how to take them!"

A prominent public-relations man told me he had

spent years at sea in the armed forces, heard all the expletives and four-letter words he thought were in existence, until he began to deal with some female clients today. He said he could hardly believe the shocking statements coming out of their mouths.

Now I ask you, is this what it means for a woman to be "liberated"? What is so desirable about acting, talking, and thinking like a man? What is so attractive about reversing sex roles?

I watched a documentary recently on television, which told about girl gangs. It was unreal. The things which are being done by females today are beyond the imagination of what we might have anticipated, even a few years ago.

The cigarette ad which proclaims, "You've come a long way, Baby!" fits the situation. However, a lot of it has been in the wrong direction. A woman friend of mine said, "I enjoy having a man walk on the outside of me for protection, and furthermore, I love having a man hold the car door and assist me getting in and out of cars." It's very dubious that women can have those courtesies, when you consider how rapidly they are losing the respect of men.

Women have contributed their time and talents to effect some great reforms in society. It has been said that woman is man's conscience. Certainly a sensitive, sincere woman can influence a man for the better, if she really cares about his moral and spiritual welfare. I believe women should undergird men with their particular talents, not undermine them.

Power in the "Little Woman"

Some females detest being called "the little woman." I was one of those years ago. Have you ever thought how mighty the influence of the "little woman" can be? While I'm not particularly keen about women preachers, God obviously calls some to the ministry. However, the Bible says each of us has a ministry, wherever we are.

I shall never forget J.C. Penney's remark in Washington, D.C., at the Religious Heritage of America banquet. When honored as Churchman of the Year (not churchperson!), he humbly and quietly remarked, "All that I am and ever will be I owe to my saintly Christian mother." Hear that, female persons? That's a tribute!

What difference does it make if we are the power behind the throne—or on it? This prominent businessman placed every laurel given to him at the feet of his mother, a woman.

Remember Esther in the Bible? She was a woman whose clear judgment and intelligence matched her beauty. Here was a simple Hebrew woman who was chosen to be queen of the greatest empire on earth at that time, the Kingdom of Persia. She discovered that intrigue was rampant in the court and that Haman, a favorite of the king, was hatching a plan to kill all the Jews. Haman was the Hitler of the Old Testament.

Queen Esther, risking her own life, revealed the plot of Haman to her husband, the king, and saved her people from certain disaster.

Esther exerted her woman power as the woman behind the throne. If she had lived today, she probably would have tried to initiate a *coup d'etat* and taken over the throne herself!

Why are women today trying to take away from men their right to lead?

Roy and I were in London to appear on the popular "Muppet Show." We were getting a little exercise between rehearsals by taking a brisk walk up the Strand. We passed a young Japanese couple, and I noticed that the man was walking quite a bit ahead of the woman, as is the custom in some countries. She was not in the least perturbed, but serenely smiling.

I have never particularly cottoned to this tradition. In fact, I found myself bristling at the sight. However, after considering the astounding divorce rate in America (in comparison with that of Japan), my bristles started to subside. If a woman is content to walk behind her man, why incite her to dissatisfaction? We are not all temperamentally alike. What an incredibly dull world this would be otherwise! God has gifted each of us as He sees fit. Some of us may not relish the idea of taking a backseat to a man in any area. On the other hand, all the seats cannot be front ones, can they? We should remember that the winds of adversity hit harder at the front seat.

The Arrangement

Many women today are assuming a role which is old in the history of man, but rather new in its widespread modern use. Not a wife, not a mistress, but a partner in a so-called arrangement. It is not easy for me to understand what is called the "living-together arrangement." It would appear that *commitment* is a word which is fast disappearing from human consciousness. This sort of relationship used to be a hush-hush topic, a target for gossip and conjecture. Today the columnists print the details of these liaisons openly and unabashedly.

I've heard a new term recently that I think applies to this type of relationship. The kids are saying it a lot. It's *scuzzy*.

Where is the meaning in a live-in arrangement? These people just want the icing off the cake. Too much icing can be sickening. I read an article recently about rules for "live-ins" and I was astounded. However, with divorce so easy to come by, it's no wonder these arrangements are so popular. "Why bother with divorce? We'll just shack up and enjoy frivolous sex, until our divergent paths and individual personalities begin to rub, and then we'll split!" No hard feelings—that's that!

Wait a minute. It can be very traumatic, no matter what a woman says about freewheeling sex and shared-living quarters, when the relationships become chilled. A woman feels betrayed. She may not admit it, even to herself, but it's there. Perhaps this comes from centuries of tradition, but I feel that she subconsciously feels that she has broken the moral law of God, the law of love, and has betrayed her birthright as a woman.

It really doesn't matter to me if some laugh at me and say, "How square can you get?" Believe me, there may come a day when they look at these things in a different light—maybe when it happens to their own daughters.

Most of us do not want our daughters to repeat our mistakes.

But, look, I can't judge anyone. God has the last word and always will, for He is God. When we miss the mark of His standards we are sinners—it's as simple as that. His standards are for man and woman to live together in holy alliance, not in unholy defiance. The Bible says that God is not mocked (Galatians 6:7). These living-together affairs are mockeries of the man-woman relationship.

Women's Rights (or Wrongs)

Everywhere I go in my travels I'm hearing about women's rights, women's fight for equality. I'm not sure how the whole women's-lib movement got started, but I have certainly questioned the direction in which it has gone. Now it seems that some of the leaders of the movement are beginning to question themselves.

With great joy, I noted comments from some prominent members of the feminist movement in the February 6, 1979, issue of the *National Enquirer*. On the front page, in bold letters was written: WOMEN'S LIB LEADERS ADMIT: WE WERE WRONG. The article has the banner headline:

WOMEN'S LIB LEADERS ADMIT THEY WERE WRONG ABOUT MARRIAGE, MOTHERHOOD, BEAUTY, AND MEN.

I had to express a silent *Hooray!* as I was reading. Representative Shirley Chisholm (D-NY) stated:

The movement's early efforts to broaden the horizons and open alternatives to women left the role of the housewife out in the cold. Thus, women were made to feel apologetic for being only housewives. But now the movement says it's perfectly O.K. to be a housewife and wear makeup and dress the way you feel.

Jo-Anne Budde, who six years ago founded the national organization "Housewives for ERA" told the *Enquirer:*

The women's lib leadership made a mistake in making femininity a dirty word. It was wrong because they alienated the traditional housewife. We peg homemakers in our society as dull and uninteresting people and that's wrong.

Betty Friedan, the mother of the women's movement and author of *The Feminine Mystique* said, "This period of rejecting motherhood and housework is now over." She added:

In the beginning, women in the movement were ready to throw out the baby with the bathwater, to act out of rage in disregarding their traditional roles and styles of dress. They now realize they're denying themselves something important when they deny their softness, prettiness, nurturing ability, earthiness, and domestic qualities . . . all the things that have been part of the traditional women's image.

Ms. Friedan (I am sure she would prefer *Ms.*), the first president of the National Organization for Women (NOW), said the most vocal leaders of the movement "had gone too far with their loud rhetoric about housework and dress styles. They copped out, ignoring the real needs of women today—husbands, homes, jobs, and many other problems."

Phyllis Schlafly, who is leading the fight against ERA, said:

> At first the women's movement tried to put housewives down. The leaders painted the housewife as the most menial, degraded, and imprisoned of all creatures. They gave the housewife an inferiority complex. Recently, the movement took a new tack. One proof of that is that the 100,000 members of NOW elected as president a housewife from Pittsburgh with a husband and children.

My first reaction to all this was, "Girls, you are locking the barn too late; the horses are out." Then I thought of the years I wrestled with the seeming injustice to women. This was before I came to grips with the fact that womanhood is wonderful, with great rewards. Even if some of the horses are out, it's not too late to round them up again and show them the home corral isn't so bad after all.

Not every woman can take public life. I had to laugh when I read a statement made by a woman politician to other women in public life: "If you can't take the heat, get back in the kitchen." Believe me, not every woman can take the heat of a very fickle public. Some women are particularly gifted and suited for professional and public life, but many are just as gifted and suited for the homemaker role, and *both* are needed in today's society.

Businesswoman, But Always a Woman

Recently I was privileged to address twelve hundred women of Home Interiors in San Francisco. I told of the power of God in my life, and saluted His power in their lives and their business of teaching women to beautify the home. As I sat at breakfast, there were several of those women waiting for their delightful mentor, Mary Crowley of Dallas, to speak at that day's session in the seminar. What an inspiration she brings to her sales force! Mary Crowley, head of the organization, is, in my opinion, a giantess of a Christian, towering as a businesswomen in her influence.

She exemplifies and fulfills the apostle John's wish for the followers of Jesus: "Beloved, I pray that in all respects you may prosper and be in good health, just as your soul prospers" (3 John 2).

Mary Crowley proves that you cannot outgive God. Like the late, beloved Henrietta Mears, Mary is a tremendous source of Christian encouragement, particularly to women. Her energies are obviously channeled into the stream of God's great current of spiritual power. She has learned, women, to keep her priorities straight, and it is paying off.

The Bible has its businesswomen, and they are vivid examples to us of how women can pursue a career outside the home. Lydia was a very successful saleswoman, having a business of "selling purple," which was a unique purple dye used in the clothing of the upper-class citizens of her city.

She was a Jewess who worshiped God, but accepted Jesus Christ as her Messiah through the ministry of the apostle Paul. When she became a Christian, we are told that she always had open house for other believers and became known as a hospitable and gracious hostess. She had her priorities straight. She was, first of all, a devoted Christian, and then a hard-working businesswoman, who continued to sell her purple dyes for God's glory.

Separate, But Equal

I happen to believe that a woman is entitled to equal pay for equal qualifications and performance. There have been inequities in this department, and I realize this. However, if I were considering hiring a man or a woman who were equally qualified for a job, and the man had a family with a nonworking wife, while the woman applicant was single, or had no children to support, I would be inclined to hire the man who needed to support his family. I don't think this is sexual discrimination.

If the man were single and the woman a single parent, I would tend to hire the woman, because of the needs of the children.

Women, we aren't all the same. Some women are born homemakers, domestically inclined and oriented. They should be lauded, not demeaned. Their occupation is tremendously demanding, but probably the most rewarding of all. Her works "praise her in the gates of the city" (*see* Proverbs 31:31). The most important works are her children, who come after her. To nurture and shape a young life to meet confidently the challenges of a swiftly changing world is, to me, the ultimate of achievement for a woman or a man. Whoops, did I say *man*, too? Is this a role reversal? I don't believe so. I see nothing wrong with a man helping with the children and the housework, particularly if both parents work outside the home. It's pretty difficult for me to understand a man opting to completely reverse his role, being the homemaker, while his wife goes out to work, unless, of course, he is disabled. However there may be exceptions to that rule, also.

Children are just as much a part of the man as the woman; the male image, as well as the female, is crucial for the full development of the children.

When it comes to the home and the children, I do not believe that a tally sheet should be kept on the things a man and a woman do within the family. As for women, we are not less than man, we are part of man and man is part of us.

Woman is the feminine of man. We were not only created to be man's helper, but also his complement. Throughout history men, either through pride or moral perversion, have mistreated women. The ancient world was predominantly a man's world. But in the nation of Israel, the Jews held women in high esteem.

However, it was Christ who truly set women free, who gave them a status equal with man, but separate from manliness. It has been Christianity which has freed women from second-class citizenship. All the laws, regulations, and ordinances which are being introduced into our society today could be eliminated, if women only realized that man-made rules are not going to give us the satisfaction, joy, and inner peace which we desire. Women, lay aside your banners and quiet your shouting voices. Listen to the quiet, assuring voice of Jesus Christ.

> And He said to the woman,"Your faith has saved you; go in peace."
>
> Luke 7:50

6
Rock and Rule

A woman is raised into a new sphere of importance when she becomes a mother. True, responsibilities are multiplied, but so are the joys. Her role in life may become either enhanced or enslaved, and sometimes it is a combination of both. The emotion which predominates is her choice.

A few years ago a woman wrote a book called *Mother's Day Is Over*. In it, this mother, Shirley Radl, said:

> Many women come to feel, as I do, that the scales of motherhood do not really balance out for them, that the rewards of motherhood—and they are indeed there, and nothing here is meant to suggest otherwise—are not great enough to offset the difficulties and plain unpleasantness of so much of the job.

Sure it's a difficult job. But is it worth it?

Elton John, the popular rock "superstar" is quoted as saying that he believed motherhood to be the most important, rewarding experience a woman can have. Now I realize, Elton, that you are speaking from observation, but as one who speaks from firsthand knowledge, I would add, *Right on!*

However, many today are saying that motherhood is overrated, and the presence of mother is not vital to the welfare of the young child. I have heard some very persuasive talk about the need for government-controlled child-care centers. This is a frightening specter of George Orwell's *Nineteen Eighty-Four*. Other writers are saying that women need to shed guilt over leaving their children for a career outside the home.

If the importance of motherhood is exaggerated, why do many top obstetricians immediately place the newborn on the mother's stomach? Why have "lying-in hospitals," where the baby rooms with the mother, become so important?

There is a school of thought which declares that mothers who give their babies up for adoption experience severe emotional problems later. It is also said that these babies, if institutionalized in either a hospital or an orphange for appreciable lengths of time, suffer deep-seated emotional trauma, which sometimes surfaces in teen years. I can attest to this, having been a foster as well as an adoptive mother. The question is eventually asked, "Why was I put up for adoption?"

You might ask me, "You were left with a baby to support—why didn't you put him out for adoption?" I have had to explain that my mother came to my aid. Even then, because I had to leave my son for long periods in my work and career, there was mental anxiety suffered by both of us. My son's emotional needs, plus the Christian love and training of my mother, led him to a complete commitment to Jesus Christ at the age of ten. Had this not happened, my son's story might have been vastly different. You see, women, I'm not just "flapping my gums" about this. You are getting it from the horse's mouth. I've been there.

I sorely missed the experience of my son's toddling years, his first ball game, of being the one to personally buy his first "knee-pant suit." I was in an office (of necessity) struggling to get into show business (not of necessity) in those years. I remember how I cried over my little boy's absence when I left him with my mother, traveling to Chicago to try to break into show business. Later on there was the joy and difficulty of trying to keep him with me, only to return him to my mother because of too little money and time to look after his needs adequately. He came to me permanently when he was twelve, when I was finally able to support him. Because of his childhood experiences and his Christian commitment, today he is an exemplary husband and father. God has wonderfully and abundantly rewarded his faith by giving to him what he missed as a child: a family of his own. Thank You, Lord!

Her Children Bless Her

I was no more than a child myself when my first baby was born. It took me a long time to learn how to be a mother, and then I guess the Lord gave me about every conceivable challenge to test me.

Some women seem to be especially gifted as mothers, wives, and homemakers. One woman, whose family was made famous in the book *Cheaper by the Dozen*, was Lillian Gilbreth. She was probably the foremost industrial engineer of her day, and she incorporated the time-and-motion studies (which she and her husband had designed to be used in factories) in her home. Most women would be aghast at the prospect of running a household with twelve children under one roof, let alone combining these responsibilities with helping a husband in his business.

Lillian Gilbreth became a widow when she was only forty-six and faced the prospect of carrying on her husband's work—*and* keeping the huge family intact. She went on to teach, write books, and leave her imprint on our society through the motion-study courses she established throughout the world.

What an explosion of influence many great mothers have kindled in this world! The fires they have built have warmed generations of children and grandchildren.

Susanna Wesley

Few mothers in history have possessed the spiritual strength and God-inspired wisdom as Susanna Wesley. This remarkable mother had nineteen children, which was not uncommon in the seventeenth century. The hardships and heartaches, which plagued her life, could have overwhelmed her. Instead she found a constant source of strength in God and was rewarded by being the mother of John Wesley, the founder of Methodism, and Charles Wesley, the hymn writer who composed more than three thousand hymns, many of which we sing today.

I was amazed, when I read about the trials Susanna

Wesley faced. Only nine of her nineteen children lived to be adults. One child smothered in his sleep, twins died, her first daughter died, another daughter was deformed for life. The family home burned twice; once they were left with only two pieces of charred paper. They lived on the edge of poverty, with debts so large that Susanna's husband had to go to jail.

Most modern women would have retreated to their beds with tranquilizers, if they encountered any one of the problems which beset Susanna Wesley. What did she do? She spent six hours a day for twenty years teaching her children. In addition, she secluded herself for two hours each day to pray and read the Bible.

So often today we hear women say, "I just don't have time." The more I read about Susanna Wesley, the harder I searched to find out if God had given her more than twenty-four hours in a day. He didn't. She had exactly the same time as I have, and you have. Here is what she advised her eldest son Samuel:

> . . . Begin and end the day with Him who is the Alpha and Omega, and if you really experience what it is to love God, you will redeem all the time you can for His more immediate service.

Quoted by Edith Deen in
Great Women of the Christian Faith

Mother of the Salvation Army

Catherine Booth was another amazing mother. She had eight children, but even more remarkable was the great army she mothered, which extends around the world and numbers in the millions. She was literally the mother of the Salvation Army. Through all her years of unselfish service, Catherine was not a strong woman physically. She was afflicted with curvature of the spine from childhood and had symptoms of tuberculosis.

How indebted we are to the mothers who have influenced our world with their devotion and unselfishness.

Grandmother Wood

My own blessed maternal grandmother, Esther Octavia Wood, is someone who left her mark upon me, although she died when I was seven. I can remember her vividly to this day. My clearest memory of her is sitting on the screened back porch of the family home in Uvalde, Texas, on a hot day, churning milk, singing hymns, with her Bible and *Baptist Standard* nearby. "Mama Wood," as I called her, was plump, pretty, with iron-gray hair swept back in a pompadour. She had clear, kind eyes that blessed whomever she surveyed. She bore eight children, first a boy, followed by seven girls.

She made a lasting impression on me, when I visited her in the hospital in San Antonio, two days before her death. She was facing a ruptured gall-bladder operation, and her smile was sweet as the kiss of an angel. Before they took her by train from Uvalde to the hospital, she looked up, smiled, as she said, "I'm ready, if God wants to take me." Then she asked her older girls to take care of her fourteen-year-old "baby."

In her casket she was breathtakingly beautiful to a seven-year-old grandchild. It was hard to believe she was not humanly alive. There was never a doubt in my mind that her destination was heaven. She was a wonderful mate to my grandfather, and a beautiful, dedicated mother to her children. She was willing to be used of God in her church, neighborhood, and community.

It Started With Eve

Eve was the "mother of all the living," which was Adam's name for her. Did he anticipate that quality within her? Eve had not given birth to the first child, when she was named as the one who would be life-giving. Her life is in all of us.

How paradoxical that Eve was created to be Adam's "helpmeet," only to do him in by enticing him to partake of the forbidden fruit! By the way, the term "helpmeet" gives a woman her true position in the world. It's only in Christianity that woman is the helper, or equal of man.

But Satan found Eve's vulnerable spot and pounced. Wasn't pride her downfall, just as it was Lucifer's descent? Lucifer wanted to be above God; he wanted to *be* God! When God pronounced judgment upon the once-perfect Lucifer, Satan came into existence. When Satan promised Eve that the forbidden fruit would make the pair wise as gods, able to discern good and evil, Eve gave in to his temptations, and sin came into the world.

Okay, but why did Adam succumb to the tempting of Eve? He must have been very enamored of his helpmeet, as well as trusting her, instead of God's command, to abstain from the fruit.

Because of Eve, all creation fell under the curse of rebellion. Because of Eve, woman has borne children in great travail. Because of Eve, Adam had to toil by the sweat of his brow to eke out a living.

And yet, by the heel of Eve, the head of the serpent was bruised. Through a woman, God's perfect universe was polluted, and yet, through a woman, a perfect salvation has been provided for all the sinning generations of children to follow that first family.

In Saint Nicholas Episcopal Church in Encino, California, where we were members for a time, there is a magnificent painting of Mary holding the Christ Child. She is standing on the head of the serpent, which is symbolic of the satanic powers that Eve's transgression brought into the world, and that Christ—through His death on the Cross—put under His feet.

God must have loved and trusted woman, to send His only begotten Son through her to redeem a hostile and uncaring world. Jehovah God could have manifested Himself in the Person of His Son any way He chose. He didn't need woman to bear the Anointed One, but He chose her, just as the prophet Isaiah predicted (Isaiah 7:14). An awesome honor, indeed, women.

Furthermore, He could have chosen a queen, a woman of lofty esteem in the eyes of the world. Instead, He chose a very young, obscure virgin: Mary, the mother of our Lord.

The Most-honored Mother

In November, after our little "Angel Unaware," Robin Elizabeth, left us, God gave me some heartfelt lyrics to the ever-beautiful and soul-inspiring "Ave Maria." We women should love and revere her, for she was part of the redemptive process in the saving of our souls. She was the instrument of God's grace for bearing the Savior of mankind. I have always believed she was very, very special, to have been chosen of God and to say *yes* to the angel Gabriel. "I am the Lord's servant, and I am willing to do whatever he wants. May everything you said come true . . ." (Luke 1:38 LB). The King James Version, in its unique beauty says, ". . . be it unto me according to thy word."

My song is:

> *Ave Maria;* Full of Grace, blessed art thou
> Among women, thou are the highest,
> For thou wast chosen of God to bear
> The wondrous Savior of the world,
> Blessed Jesus, my Lord—
> Many sorrows pierced thy dear heart,
> But thou wast faithful to the end—
> I long to follow thy example—
> Blessed Mother, Mother of Jesus, my Lord,
> *Ave, Maria!*

These lyrics were approved by Cardinal McIntyre of the Los Angeles Diocese of the Catholic Church and I recorded them in a "Little Golden Record," with Roy's "The Lord's Prayer" on the other side. I was privileged to sing these words at a Catholic funeral and a wedding.

Mary has been the best-known woman in the history of the world. No other woman has been so honored as a mother. I've often thought of the years she spent raising her Son, knowing all the time that He was the promised

Messiah. No woman has kept a more important secret.

What kind of a mother was she? We are not told about the childhood, adolescence, and young manhood of Jesus, but we do note that He "kept increasing in wisdom and stature, and in favor with God and men" (Luke 2:52). From His human side, Jesus was under the parental influence of Joseph and Mary. Mary gave Jesus a home filled with love and mutual understanding. She cared for His physical needs, carefully preparing the food which would give Him the strength He needed for His future rigorous life.

Mary was obedient to God and taught her Son obedience. We know that the Old Testament was in that home and that Mary's mind must have been full of its prophecies and promises.

I have known the pain of losing children, but I can only imagine one small part of the agony Mary must have experienced in those last three-and-a-half years of her Son's life.

How Jesus loved her! In His last hour on the Cross, He gave His mother to the beloved disciple John. Her heart must have broken in a thousand pieces, as she watched her sinless, loving Son in His agony. She knew His destiny, but she was also human. What a very remarkable woman she must have been.

How God honored woman, through Mary!

Pope John Paul II declared in no uncertain terms that motherhood is woman's vocation. One can almost hear the cries of protest from many lib quarters. Try as we will, women, we cannot deny the mothering instinct. If we do not mother our own offspring, then we will mother a younger brother or sister. Sometimes we even mother our husbands!

Mother, you are the heart of the home. Don't ever forget how important you are!

7
The Found Generation

As I write this I'm sitting in my room on the thirty-first floor of the Sheraton Hotel in Toronto, Canada. I'm here to witness and sing at a fund-raising dinner for a Christian school. At breakfast in the coffee shop a woman sitting opposite me asked, "What brings you all the way to Toronto from Los Angeles for one night?"

So many people wonder why I scoot around the country doing one-night public appearances. I imagine that some of the people probably add under their breath, "At her age, too!" Well, let me tell you what I said to that woman in Toronto.

I told her how vital the Christian school is to our very survival as a free people. Women, if we lose this generation of youngsters to atheistic thinking, we will lose the freedoms we have long enjoyed. Let us make no mistake about it. We will either be subject to Almighty God and His Commandments, which insure individual freedom and dignity, or we will be tyrannized by man with his ever-changing whims and devious humanistic schemes.

Humanity, of itself, has no ethical standards. This has been provided by God—Madalyn Murray O'Hair notwithstanding.

Today we're hearing a lot in the schools about teaching "values." I'm not sure whose values set the standard for the instruction. If we depend upon the secular school to give our children spiritual training, we are definitely barking up the wrong tree.

Training should begin in the home, before the child even starts to nursery school. Psychologists and psychiatrists know what they're talking about when they say the first five years are a crucial period in a child's life.

Let us consider a child who has had no spiritual training at home. The little boy or girl is thrust into the secular school, with Mother relieved that she finally has him or her out from underfoot. For a few hours a day, the teacher can take over. And that's exactly what happens. Secularism starts to crystallize in the child's thinking. Some children have never heard the name *God* or *Jesus*—except as profanity.

Is it any wonder that we see the rise of dope, alcoholism, rape, burglary, kidnapping, and murder by the young? I recently read about the rise in crime by children of elementary-school age.

Rights of Children

Woman, what is your priority in life? Is it to do your own thing, or help the young find their way to God? The beloved Corrie ten Boom tells about her childhood so poignantly in her book *In My Father's House*. She relates the story of her mother praying with her, when she invited Jesus into her heart. She was only five years old at the time. She writes:

> Does a child of five really know what he's doing?
> Some people say that children don't have
> spiritual understanding—that we should wait
> until a child can "make up his mind for himself."
> I believe a child should be led, not left to wan-
> der.

How very true! And yet how many children are left to
wander! Their minds are not guided toward the things
of God, but toward the comics, television, and the
things of the world. They are left to wander in this vast
area of godless thinking.

I absolutely cringe when I hear someone say, "I don't
want to force my child into church. I want him to be able
to decide for himself." Would a parent let a child enter a
busy intersection without guidance? Why then should a
child be permitted to approach the dangers of living in
this freewheeling world without divine guidance?

Too many children today are like planets which have
whirled out of orbit. They are spinning in space without
gravitational pull.

Do children have rights? Everyone is concerned about
women's rights, minority rights, and every other conceivable type of rights, but what about the children? I
believe children have the *right* to hear about God. They
have the *right* to love and encouragement.

Mommy, I'm Afraid of the Dark!

What can we do to give our children a feeling of security? Inner security begins in the cradle. We can begin
by being there with them whenever possible. They

learn to love very early, nestled in a mother's arms, held close to her breast. We can speak the truth of God's love to an infant, and it will be recorded in his subconscious mind.

The first song I can remember learning from my mother was "Jesus Loves Me," and then she taught me "Jesus Loves the Little Children of the World." Both songs bore fruit in my middle years, when I gave myself to the loving Jesus, and again when we adopted children of other races.

We can teach our children to talk to God in an uninhibited fashion. When our children were living at home, we had a family altar (actually an old console), where I encouraged them to pray and tell Jesus about their problems and thank Him for their blessings. The altar was the focal point of the living room. At one time this console held a radio, television, and a record-player, but years and better equipment had rendered it obsolete. However, it made a very adequate place of worship!

I had different coverings with which I draped the console at different times of the year, and had the girls pick flowers to brighten it. We had an antique New England kneeling bench, covered with petit point, in front of this makeshift altar. Sometimes when the children were praying, I would kneel down beside them; other times I would respect their desire to be alone with the Lord. This little altar is still with us here in Apple Valley, and the memories it conveys are sweet indeed.

Our organ sat at the opposite side of the room, and next to it was a glass door leading to the patio. In one of the panels of the door we placed a lovely picture of Jesus. When the light shined through the door, it illuminated the picture and lit up the whole room.

We can honestly let our children know that parents have problems, too, but that God helps us and forgives us when we stumble. He is faithful and can be depended upon, when no one else is there; He is interested in the smallest happenings of our lives, as well as the great ones.

Several years ago, I wrote our daughters a Mother's Day letter, encouraging them to give their children the one true security—a vital relationship to God through Jesus Christ. I tried to point out that though they gave their children material things, those things would never comfort and sustain them in the deep valleys of their lives. Only eternity will reveal what, if anything, my letter accomplished.

As a mother, I did the best I could with the light given to me in raising the children. I'm sure I made many mistakes, but God knows how hard I tried. I tried to set a right example in giving them true standards and, by God's grace, to maintain them myself. Our children had plenty of love to balance the necessary discipline, and it takes both.

I would not trade my experiences in motherhood for the position of Chairwoman of the Board of the largest corporation in the world.

Priorities

Woman, what is your priority in life? Is it to do your thing, or to help the young find their way to the Lord, who created them?

To be a mother is hard, tedious, and demanding. But

it is wonderfully rewarding. Let's look again at the woman in Proverbs 31. The woman depicted here was very busy. She got up early in the morning to prepare food for her family and to start her large household humming. She sewed for the family, shopped, and had a business on the side. In addition, she had a warm and compassionate heart, caring for the poor and needy.

I'm really amazed at this woman, because it says that she also made linen garments and sold them. She was evidently well dressed herself, because it is said that "Her clothing is fine linen and purple" (v. 22).

The crowning achievement of this woman is that "Her children rise up and bless her . . ." (v. 28). That, woman, is achievement in the highest.

Being a successful career woman is commendable. Having an attractive home and cooking fine meals are plus points on anyone's chart. But raising a child "in the way he should go" and nurturing a love for God in his heart is a truly creative accomplishment. You have faithfully tended the young plant into blossoming and bearing fruit. This is life—ongoing, rich, and beautiful.

Mother First

If the priorities of a mother have been self-serving only, then her tree will look bare, indeed. The branches will be dry and lifeless, instead of fragrant and abundant. What happens when women succumb to the wiles of the Tempter about self-indulgence? One ghastly result of our letting down the bars of vigilance in protecting our young is the onslaught of sex exploiters.

You may think I'm talking of extremes, but I think it's

time we realize the propaganda we are getting about all the aspects of self-centeredness. If women are focused on self, who is tending to the children?

Last night when I switched on the television I was aghast at the coming attractions of the late-night sex pictures. It was hard to believe we would allow such filth to be advertised over the airwaves. Those coming-attraction flyers were disgusting—an insult to humanity.

I couldn't help wondering what kind of homes spawned those boy and girl "stars of porno." Who are the mothers and fathers who have been so stripped of any human decency that they would allow their children to be destroyed by purveyors of filth and human degradation?

Jesus told His disciples that it was inevitable that people would put stumbling blocks in the path of righteousness, but He gave this solemn warning: ". . . woe to him through whom they [the stumbling blocks] come! It would be better for him if a millstone were hung around his neck and he were thrown into the sea, than that he should cause one of these little ones to stumble" (Luke 17: 1,2).

It is not only the satanic influence of the makers of the child-porno films and publishers of books, but even more the *parents* of these poor, exploited children who are responsible.

I was recently reading about a conference, which is being held in my state, on the needs of children. Now I have nothing against conferences, except when the answers to the problems are laid on the steps of government. All the government regulations in the world will not lead a little child to the knowledge and love of Jesus Christ.

In my book *Hear the Children Crying*, I talked about the ultimate wickedness of child abuse. Abuse takes many forms, but I would like to restate what I said in that book:

> It is well-nigh impossible for any child to come unto Jesus Christ and to love God and man, under such treatment. To me, one of the saddest sights in this world is that of a child robbed of his potential of faith in a God who loves him. I have come to believe with all my heart that we must fight such robbery of childhood with all that is within us.

His Eye on the Sparrow

It is now 7:00 A.M. I am gazing out my dining-room window here in Apple Valley, into the sun-drenched desert scene. Large trees in the backyard, freshly pruned of deadwood, are starkly etched against a cloudless sky. The hope of spring stirs gently within me. As I look closely, I can see fragile shoots reaching from the tops of the cut limbs.

Morning in the desert is soothing to me. Without intrusion of a loud and harsh world, the simplicity of God's creation is so real. As I look at those trees, I wonder where the birds will nest this spring. There is so little foliage to camouflage their nests. It's funny, though, I've seen birds nesting in the prickly cactus bushes in front of our house. My skin crawls when I think of babies being hatched in those nests. What if the tiny fledglings should fall into those razor-edge stickers? Do you know that I have never seen a little dead baby bird in that cactus?

Isn't God terrific? The way He provides, guides, and protects His young—even birds—never fails to amaze me. The Bible says not a sparrow shall fall without His knowing (Matthew 10:29).

We women, as mothers, must instill in our young very strong faith in the God of the universe. We must teach them early—very early—that He is everywhere, all-seeing, all-loving, all-knowing, and all-powerful. Our little ones deserve to know that He cares about every aspect of their lives.

The love for Jesus and the absolute trust in the face of a child is a treasure beyond measure.

To give a child faith in Jesus is far more precious than the most expensive worldly gift a mother or father might tender. This gift is eternal.

8
An Unborn Child

Until recently there were some subjects which were hush-hush in all but medical circles. However, in the past few years, one of those topics has been the center of political, social, and religious controversy. We can't ignore it when we're talking to women. In some ways it touches all our lives. Women, what do you believe about abortion? Are you for or against? Eventually we must declare our position.

The dictionary defines the word *abortion*: "Expulsion of a fetus from the womb before it is sufficiently developed to survive." *Fetus* is defined as "the offspring in the womb from the end of the third month of pregnancy until birth."

When we look at the use of words in the English language, we discover they can be used to change the meaning of an act. Dr. C. Everett Koop, chief surgeon of Children's Hospital in Philadelphia, said, "I am convinced that we are using certain words to depersonalize the unborn baby. It doesn't pose such a problem when you decide to kill it. It's easier to kill a fetus than an unborn baby" (*Christianity Today*, December 15, 1978).

If we substituted, "unborn child" every time we saw

the word *fetus*, we might get a different perspective on the subject of abortion.

Woman is designed to bear children. When a woman becomes pregnant, everything in her starts to prepare for nurturing and carrying a child to term in pregnancy. From a purely biological standpoint, I believe abortion is destructive to the woman, because it halts a very fast development within her. It is contrary to nature.

It's significant that some cancer specialists believe women who nurse their babies are less apt to develop breast cancer than those who take pills to dry up. Perhaps this is a poor parallel, but in my honest opinion there are unpleasant effects, physical, mental, and spiritual to abortion.

First of all, there is the guilt trauma. Somehow a woman feels she has foiled and failed her womanhood in aborting her child. Years ago, when abortion was illegal, many women died from infection. Today there is less danger, physically, since abortion is legal in many areas. A Christian doctor said, "Just because it's legal doesn't make it right."

However, there is no real way of telling what long-term damage abortion does to a woman physically, particularly when she has more than one. Today, where it is legal, some women have come to depend upon abortion as a form of birth control, and see it as something no worse than taking the "pill."

Dr. Koop said, "If you don't have a last-ditch therapy such as abortion, then people pay a little bit more attention to their techniques of contraception. In places like Czechoslovakia, Poland, and Japan, people have gotten less and less careful about true contraception, because they know that if they do get pregnant, they always have a way out in abortion."

Freewheeling sex outside of wedlock most certainly is not helping to curb abortion. I have known women who have had abortions and then found it next to impossible to conceive or carry a child when they wanted a family.

But My Husband Insisted

I knew a woman who was coerced by her husband into having an abortion. He said they couldn't afford another child. They had only one child, but he thought one more would put such a strain on them that they couldn't survive. She pleaded with him to let her carry the baby, saying, "God will provide for us." It was useless. He was adamant. After the abortion, the woman said she inwardly despised her husband. She felt that she had violated her own body and taken the life of her unborn child. The marriage ended in divorce.

In another case it wasn't a husband, but parents who insisted that a girl have an abortion. A teenage girl had become pregnant and wanted to marry the father of her child. Both his parents and her parents decided they were too young, and that she should have an abortion. The girl was pathetic in her desire to carry the child, but had to give in to the pressure. I saw her several weeks later. She cried and said she was terribly depressed. She felt that she had committed a serious sin and asked me to pray for her.

Later, the girl saw a television special on abortion, in which a pile of aborted fetuses was shown. The pictures were taken in the same hospital where she had gone. She wondered if one of the little bodies was her aborted child, and was unable to think about it without crying. I have no idea what the emotional results will be for this young girl.

A More Positive Side

I was on a panel television show when a woman called in with a story that touched me deeply. She had taken the drug thalidomide and was told by doctors to abort her baby because the child would be horribly deformed. Someone gave her a copy of *Angel Unaware*, and after reading it, she decided she would trust God and have the baby.

This grateful mother called me, because she wanted me to know her little girl was born perfect. She thanked me for writing about our little Robin Elizabeth, who was here on earth only two years and yet changed our lives. The woman said, "If I had listened to all the frightening stories about abnormal children and gone through with the abortion, I would never have known the blessing of my beautiful little girl."

Are There Exceptions?

There are pros and cons about the issue, and no one case is exactly the same as another. However, the Bible says, "Thou shalt not kill," and there is penalty somewhere, sometime for killing.

God is not mocked, and we shouldn't kid ourselves about this. He sees all and knows all. This is not to say

He will not forgive, if one is truly repentant. This is what the Cross is all about.

I cannot understand anyone aborting after the end of three months, legal or not, unless something happens in the pregnancy where the mother's life is in jeopardy.

In the case of rape or incest, I believe the woman should be taken care of immediately, for if a pregnancy should develop, that little unborn child, having been conceived by violence in rape, or by deception of the incestuous parent, faces a pretty dim future. Many criminals have this kind of background. Such a child as this has been conceived in conditions contrary to the loving creativity of God.

Many times when a woman has aborted a child because she didn't want it, or the man didn't, she later begins to wonder what she gave up. Was it a boy or girl? If he or she had lived, who would the child resemble? I meet many women who have opened their hearts to me, knowing that I will not divulge their secret guilt feelings. I know that abortion is not the will of God, and that there is penalty somewhere along the line.

I'm Not Shockproof

Not long ago I was horrified to hear an author say on television that he believed children as young as six years old should be allowed to have sex. He said that they should be instructed in it! He declared, "If the two children involved decide they want to go all the way in the sex act, then both sets of parents should consent and the children should be instructed as to the right way."

A woman in the audience said "I would kill anyone who would encourage my six-year-old to do that!"

I wanted to jump right in and say "Hooray for you, sister!" This is where we have arrived in our godless permissiveness.

Sex is beautiful when love, responsibility, and marriage are involved. Some people would relegate sex to nothing more than biological fulfillment. They disregard the spiritual aspect, which has been God-given for procreation; or they underrate the need to merge with another human being out of a feeling of love and respect.

When sex is purely self-gratification, with no feeling of responsibility for the act, it is degradation.

What feelings can a six-year-old have for another six-year-old in the sex act? As far as I am concerned, anyone who would permit or suggest this to children is just as bad as those who would photograph perverted acts for profit.

Is There an Alternative?

Abortion is sad, for so many reasons. In my book, it should only be considered in the most dire, bizarre, and impossible situations.

There are many childless couples who desire to adopt, love, and raise a baby. If at all possible, a woman who is unwed, or unable to raise a child alone, should carry the child and place it for adoption.

Here is where Christians can be of great help. If we understand the grace of God, we should extend our help and love to those girls who have the courage to have their babies, even in the face of the worldly trend toward destructive abortion.

Adoption is God's way. He invented the idea and we are all adopted. The Bible says, ". . . we should behave like God's very own children, adopted into the bosom of his family. . . ." (Romans 8:15 LB).

Where do you stand on this subject? Are you firm enough in your convictions about the worth of a human life? This is one of the biggest issues facing women today. It could affect generations to come.

9
An Undone Marriage

Let's talk about divorce. Not a pretty subject, I know, but one which we confront every day in the real world.

For years I worried about my background of divorce and remarriage. Every time I picked up the Bible, my eyes seemed to rivet on what Jesus said in Matthew 5:31,32:

> "And it was said, 'WHOEVER DIVORCES HIS WIFE, LET HIM GIVE HER A CERTIFICATE OF DISMISSAL'; but I say to you that every one who divorces his wife, except for the cause of unchastity, makes her commit adultery; and whoever marries a divorced woman commits adultery."

There it is. Rough. For a divorced person, confronting the Scriptures can be very convicting.

In the Gospel of Mark, the Pharisees were testing Jesus on His view of a man divorcing his wife. Jesus answered them:

> "What did Moses command you?" And they said, "Moses permitted a man to write a certifi-

cate of divorce and send her away." But Jesus said to them, "Because of your hardness of heart he wrote you this commandment. But from the beginning of creation, God MADE THEM MALE AND FEMALE. FOR THIS CAUSE A MAN SHALL LEAVE HIS FATHER AND MOTHER, AND THE TWO SHALL BECOME ONE FLESH; consequently they are no longer two, but one flesh. What therefore God has joined together, let no man separate."

Mark 10:3-9

Sound familiar? Those are the words of the marriage vows. The traditional ceremony says, "Let no man put asunder." Many couples are changing those vows today to conform to their own standards.

Jesus didn't sidestep any issue. When His disciples asked more questions about divorce, He said to them:

"Whoever divorces his wife and marries another woman commits adultery against her; and if she herself divorces her husband, and marries another man, she is committing adultery."

Mark 10:11

There it is again—very plain. I am one of those women who was divorced by my first husband, because he wanted to be free of responsibility. I remarried and that marriage also ended in divorce. In 1947, New Year's Eve, I married Roy Rogers, promising God there would never be another divorce in my life, regardless of circumstances. Two months later, I committed my life totally to Jesus Christ, pleading His shed blood for remission of my sins and asking Him to take over the reins of my life.

The Scars Were There

In my experience and opinion, divorce is a taste of hell. No matter how you slice it, no matter who is to blame, it can only be defined as failure to fulfill a contract between two people. In a sense, it is almost like the feeling of losing a part of yourself in death.

I have heard it said that the two most devastating events in life are the sudden death of a child—and divorce. I agree.

In divorce, for whatever the cause, there is a feeling of letting everyone down: your spouse, yourself, and, if you believe in God, letting Him down by defying His command: "What therefore God hath joined together, let not man put asunder" (March 10:9 KJV). I know, because I have had that emotion.

Once the tie is broken, one is adrift and alone in the throes of adjustment to the single life. So many times in a remarriage, there is a tendency to bring along the fears, hurts, and resentments of the previous marriage. This, coupled with a new set of emotional adjustments, makes for considerable stress on a new marital relationship.

Divorce, like war, leaves scars.

Healing

A few months after I committed my life to Christ, I was reading my Bible one day in the same chapter of

Mark 10 which had previously burdened me about my divorce, when another passage leaped out at me to give me hope.

This was the story of the rich young ruler. He came to Jesus and asked Him what he should do to inherit eternal life. Jesus quoted the Ten Commandments and the young ruler said he had followed and kept all of them. Jesus must have known the impossibility of that feat, but instead He said to him, ". . . One thing you lack: go and sell all you possess, and give it to the poor, and you shall have treasure in heaven; and come, follow Me" (Mark 10:21).

That was a tall order! The young man didn't like that idea very well because he was very rich. Now Jesus wasn't condemning money, *per se*, but what He wanted to illustrate was our inability to reach God or find peace through our own human means.

Jesus looked at His disciples and said:

> ". . . Children, how hard it is to enter the kingdom of God! It is easier for a camel to go through the eye of a needle than for a rich man to enter the kingdom of God." And they were even more astonished and said to Him, "Then who can be saved?" Looking upon them, Jesus said, "With men it is impossible, but not with God; for all things are possible with God"
>
> Mark 10:24-27

What a great truth! God, You make things possible, even impossible situations. Why should this story of the rich ruler mean so much to me? It had nothing to do with divorce and remarriage. Or did it? It made me understand again that the Law stands, but that Christ paid the penalty for our failures. The rich young man was saying, "What should I *do*?" and Jesus said, "Follow Me, I will do it all for you." This story comforted my troubled soul.

Don't misunderstand me, I'm not condoning divorce, nor trying to find a way to climb over the Law of God, or tunnel under it. The penalty of divorce is great, but Jesus can heal the wounds and give us back our health.

Jesus did not break the Law. He fulfilled it. The Law stands; nullifying God's Commandments carries penalty. However if we love the Lord, if we are truly repentant, and willing to turn from our wicked ways, He will forgive and heal our hearts, strengthen us with His Holy Spirit, and set our feet in a new, large place of service in His plan for our lives.

Wounded Children

Divorce should be the last resort in a failing marriage. Every avenue should be explored to salvage the crumbling house. The consequences can be so severe.

Look at the children. Torn between the two they love and upon whom they have depended, the children suffer severely. Some say, "It's better for a child to live with only one parent than to live with two who bicker and harbor resentment." If the situation is dire, I agree, but entirely too many people today simply get bored in their marriages and look for greener pastures. Often they find the new pastures are not as green and smooth as they first appeared. God has not promised a perennially blue sky with never a cloud. If there were no clouds, there would be no rain to refresh the earth and make things grow.

Problems in marriage should turn out to be valuable lessons for both parties. You don't quit the classroom because the subject or assignment is difficult. You study the subject to find light for the problem.

I have personally known of cases where people have stayed together "for the sake of the children." Sometimes there was no real love or respect left for each other. The children of these unions rarely appreciate this particular kind of sacrifice, for they have grown up in an unloving, tense atmosphere and carry a very dim view of marriage.

Our nation is reeling from the divorce rate. Suicides mount, child abuse abounds, dope and alcoholism result. Christians must take a stand on protecting the home, even if it means they are not happy twenty-four hours a day with their marital situation. Sometimes divorce is the only way out of an unbearable situation, but it is never desirable, because of the trauma suffered by innocent children.

Until Debts Do Us Part

But you say you couldn't possibly forgive him? Look at what he's done to you! After all you've done for him, he owes you *plenty*! Debts can be the most destructive elements in a marriage.

In addition to financial debts that one or both of you have unwisely incurred, what are some other debts that can eat at the heart of a once-healthy marriage? The worst might be the debt of infidelity. "You *owe* me—you should crawl—because your infidelity has made me so miserable, I can't forget it." Just ignore the fact that *God* forgives a truly penitent sinner; *you* simply cannot forget it.

May I submit that if you are unable to forget, you have not really forgiven the grievance. Some seem to think adultery is the Number One sin in the Bible. In the order of the Ten Commandments, it ranks number seven. One does well to remember the words of our Lord Jesus, who said in answer to a lawyer who asked "Master, which is the greatest commandment in the law?" Jesus said to him:

Thou shalt love the Lord thy God with all thy heart, and with all thy soul, and with all thy mind. This is the first and great commandment. And the second is like unto it, Thou shalt love thy neighbour as thyself. On these two commandments hang all the law and the prophets.

Matthew 22:37-40 KJV

It appears to me that many men are able to love and respect their wives, and yet lie in the arms of other women, forgetting that love, as if the act had no relation or bearing upon their marriages. Most women seem to think their husbands do not love them, if they indulge in extramarital flings. Now don't misunderstand me; I am in no way condoning marital infidelity. There is always penalty for breaking God's Commandments.

Even if one thinks he is "getting away with it," one most certainly is not. God's books are quite accurate and He misses nothing, good or bad.

Our failures, moral and spiritual, were nailed to the Cross in the Person of Jesus Christ, who took them upon His sinless self to crucify them for eternity—*if* the sinner will accept His sacrifice. What a sacrifice for us puny, miserable failing creatures!

Many marriages might be saved—*if* both parties would let go of their pride (which God abhors), ask for forgiveness, and for the grace to forgive each other for whatever indebtedness is felt. There is a certain kind of adhesive that can repair a broken utensil and make it better than it was in the first place. Almighty God has the strongest glue of all, and when He repairs anything it is powerful!

In marital conflicts sometimes someone else's pasture looks better than our own. But no field is perfect. No marriage is perfect. Jesus was, is, and always will be the only true perfection. How sad we humans can't realize that our relationships with each other are as strong as our relationship to Him in faith. It has taken me many, many years to discover and experience this truth.

But I'm a Christian, and you might say, "What about non-Christian cultures where people stay married?" That's a fair question. However, in many of those cultures the woman has generally been considered quite a cut less than the man, has accepted it without question, and lived her life in subservience to her husband. The Christian belief, according to the Bible, says that ". . . God is not one to show partiality" (Acts 10:34) and ". . . all of you who were baptized into Christ have clothed yourselves with Christ . . . there is neither male nor female . . ." (Galatians 3:27,28).

There are many little irritations between two people who have committed themselves to each other. When these little things are never resolved, never prayed about, they begin to fester into something that grows into full-scale resentment. Then one day the lid blows off. The best solution is to stop the pot from simmering *before* it begins to boil. Roy and I have made it a practice of trying "never to let the sun go down on your wrath" (*see* Ephesians 4:26).

The Church: Help or Hindrance?

A positive direction is being taken by the church in marriage counseling. The church is the very finest hospital for an ailing marriage. The Body of Christ cares— or should care—about people. Keeping the Bride of Christ healthy until the Second Coming of the Bridegroom should have top priority in God's house.

If a husband and wife would agree with a Christian marriage counselor to help in the healing of their marriage, study God's Word together, pray together, and with the help of the Holy Spirit apply His promises to the problem areas, they would have to experience a new awareness of the potential for happiness.

What about counseling for divorced and remarried persons? I'm sorry to say that many times the pastors and elders in some churches are unwilling to accept men and women into their membership who have dissolved previous marriages. Frequently the church looks askance at the union of divorced persons. Some ministers refuse to perform a marriage ceremony for them.

Only Jesus, through His atoning sacrifice and the presence of the Holy Spirit in the heart can build a solid marriage between divorced people. Some say, "Well, you can't make a silk purse out of a sow's ear." True. But listen, you can make a sturdy football from pigskin, and it can take rough handling, kicking, and still remain intact. Perhaps this is a crude analogy in regard to remarriage for divorced people, but it's the way I see it.

The trauma of divorce is considerable, but if the parties involved are willing to let God take over, He can and does take questionable material and forge a strong union that unbelievable pressures cannot break. I know.

Water in the Desert

The Bible says, ". . . In quietness and trust is your strength . . ." (Isaiah 30:15) and also, "Come away by yourselves to a lonely place and rest a while . . ." (Mark 6:31). Jesus knew we must seek solitude at times in our lives. Body, mind, and spirit need rest to regain strength. Too often we are so filled with doing that we don't take time to find out where we have been, or where we are going.

We women, if we are to be what Adam called us, "Mother of all living" (Genesis 3:20), must do what Jesus said. Periodically we need to withdraw from the hustle and bustle and be refilled ourselves. If we allow ourselves to become arid, we will have no water to refresh others who are tired, hurt, and bewildered. It's the simple law of supply and demand. God will supply, but we must open ourselves to Him, quietly, in reverence, anticipation, and gratitude.

Many people have asked why I usually travel alone to speaking and singing engagements. After years of public life, I look forward to my long drives across the desert floor to my plane flights. There are no intrusions. I can quiet the tumult of my mind. I need to tune out the opinions of others and simply listen for God to speak through that still, small voice within me.

Sometimes I need to evaluate how to react to the fickle tune of public opinion. When it's off-key, it has a tendency to jar the senses. Just recently one of the news magazines printed a prediction that Roy Rogers and Dale Evans Rogers would divorce this year because of religious differences. Another magazine predicted that we would divorce, but gave no reason. This is one of Satan's wiliest tricks. He starts a campaign to provoke controversy about those who proclaim Christ as the answer to life and its problems. Satan loves to see God's children trip and fall. In fact, he usually has his foot in the path to make us stumble.

The prediction about Roy and me pops up about every five years. It causes a little stir and dies a fairly quick death. It is possible that the rumor starts because of my traveling alone. If the rumormongers only knew that the reason our marriage has lasted almost thirty-two years is because of a mutual faith and trust in Jesus Christ, perhaps they would look elsewhere for such predictions.

I promised God the night I married Roy Rogers that there would never be a divorce, as far as I was concerned, regardless of circumstances. You see, I bear the scars of divorce, and have no stomach for it. However, the most important reason is because Christ has been so real in my life for thirty-one years, a very present help in trouble, and the Source of my joy in life. I have boldly witnessed of my faith to literally thousands of people. Divorce would be an insult to my witness.

If you would like the real inside scoop, here is the truth. (You may quote me.) I am happier now in my marriage than I have ever been. I am not speaking for my husband; I am speaking for myself. We have had our ups and downs, but over the years have learned to accept and appreciate each other. We have a good understanding, sometimes unspoken and sometimes spoken. We enjoy a good sense of humor and can laugh at ourselves. We never go to sleep with a beef between us.

Roy is less outspoken than I, but I know when to keep quiet. We enjoy traveling together, when we have to make public appearances as a team. I enjoy my husband. I really don't want to insult all the fine comics we know, but I think Roy is the funniest man alive. Some of his humor is quite earthy, but his style is so artless, and he is so much his own man that he is delightful.

Commitment is so rewarding. That's true of anything, but especially of marriage. If couples could just "wait it out" in faith and trust in the Lord, there is such a marvelous reward in the companionship of the later years.

One of the problems a man and a woman have is forgetting to be alone together while the children are growing up. Then the children leave home, and the couple doesn't even know how to talk to each other. They have forgotten to be sweethearts in the throes of raising children. I believe this accounts for many of the divorces in midlife. Roy and I were fortunate to be able to travel together in our work. We had time alone together. Our family life was very hectic, with our international family, but God always was the head of our house, then Roy, and then I.

I tried not to interfere when Roy disciplined the children, and he never challenged me, particularly in front of them. There were a few exceptions, but we both tried very hard to have a united front in discipline.

Challenges, Not Problems

Perhaps you're saying this sounds idyllic, and your circumstances are much different. Women, we may catch perfect moments in our lives, but we are living with problems every day. My friend, Carole, who is working with me on this book, refuses to talk about problems, only challenges. Perhaps that's a better way to look at life's encounters. *Challenges.*

- It is a challenge to have a marriage that lasts.

- It is a challenge to live with one person for all the days God has allotted to you on this earth.

We are to love, honor, and obey our husbands, as they follow Christ. The Bible says we are to remain with them that they may be won "without a word" (1 Peter 3:1) by our behavior. That's a tall order, women! We have the natural tendency to want to win them by talking (and maybe even preaching). I do not believe we can

ever have that winning behavior, if our husbands cannot see Christ in us. On the other hand, I do not believe
any person has the right to destroy Christian faith in his
mate. This also goes for a believing man married to an
unbelieving woman.

When one believes in Christ and the other doesn't,
this is one of the most difficult challenges. God is merci-
ful as well as just, and Christ will be our ultimate Judge.
Never, never, never give up on Jesus. If you hold on to
your faith in Him, He will rescue, spiritually resuscitate,
and strengthen you to go on, no matter how you have
failed.

He rescued me. He can give you His lifeline, too.

10
Grace to Be Graceful

Fashion is fickle, and so are women. Every season I look at the advertisements for the new trends and think, *Here we go again!* It's easy to get hung up on the latest styles. Since my personal-appearance engagements require quite a bit of thoughtful wardrobe planning, I find myself frequently concerned about what I should wear, when, and where.

The other day I must have changed my mind five times, while packing for a formal fund-raising dinner for Children's Village, USA (Beaumont, California), a facility for battered children. Following that, I had a singing and speaking stint in Grand Rapids, Michigan, for the Michigan Foster Home Association. I pulled out this outfit, and then threw it on the bed; held up another and discarded it; and then I remembered! *O dear, the kettle was boiling in the kitchen!*

I raced down the hall corridor, passing a picture of the Resurrected Christ. Instantly the words of our Lord Jesus flashed into my mind.

"And why are you anxious about clothing? Observe how the lilies of the field grow; they do not toil nor do they spin, yet I say to you that even Solomon in all his glory did not clothe himself like one of these."

Matthew 6:28,29

I thought, *Why did You bring that verse to my mind at a time like this, Lord?*

Then I remembered what Peter said about adornment being a gentle and quiet spirit, which is precious in the sight of God (1 Peter 3:4). I thought, *Woman, thy name is vanity!* I made myself a cup of instant coffee, sat down in my mother's old armchair, and picked up the Word of God. I devoured the Sermon on the Mount in Matthew 5. Believe me, my priorities began to fall in place.

Thank You Lord, for Your Word which always focuses my perspective.

Ego Buster

It's hard for someone who has been in the entertainment industry to fight the ever-surfacing ego about appearance and the opinions of others. One does well to remember that we come into this world naked, and when we leave, we can't carry perishable apparel with us.

A gifted and humorous concert pianist was asked if he ever experienced stage fright. He answered that when he felt stage fright coming on, he imagined all the people out front without a single stitch of clothes, and his fear immediately vanished. I thought that was an interesting attitude, if a bit indelicate!

Speaking of clothes, this woman really got her come-uppance the other night. I had just finished a speaking engagement in Los Angeles before about two thousand women. This has a tendency to make a person feel rather elated, especially if the audience is receptive. I went back to my hotel room and flipped on the television to have a few moments of relaxation and wind down. A young comic was telling of an experience he suffered in a club engagement at the beginning of his career. A boisterous woman was making some very loud remarks during his act. Apparently she had been imbibing a bit, and he was unable to quiet her. Finally he walked over to her table and confronted her, in an effort to get her to stop the interruptions.

The comic was relating this story to the television host, and I sat up quite straight in my bed when he said, "This gal was dressed like she was going to meet Dale Evans."

Now, what on earth did he mean by that? I wondered.

He asked the woman what she did for a living, and she answered, unabashedly, that she was a hooker.

The studio audience let loose with some loud, raucous guffaws, which is common on this particular late show. My first reaction was "*Insult!*" Then I started to laugh, remembering my frequent preoccupation with wardrobe. It took me down several pegs.

Thank, You, Lord for the grace to laugh at myself.

The Clothes Horse: From Gallop to Trot

In the *Los Angeles Times* recently, Stockard Channing, a television star, was speaking of being overly fashion conscious. She is five feet three inches tall, which is just my height. She told how she was admiring the "clothes horses" in a fashion magazine and was enamored with the way-out fashions. She began to imagine herself about five feet nine inches tall and was so inspired by this vision, that she embarked on a shopping excursion. Then she saw herself—in a full-length mirror, at that. The reality of being just five three could not be denied.

I can't count the times I have declared to some saleswoman, "Some day, the garment industry is going to wise up and design some sharp clothes for women over fifty, and under five five, and they will make millions!" And sizes . . . oh, dear! The styles seem to be designed for sizes 9, 10, 11 and even smaller! So what happens to someone like me? I wind up wearing separates and having dresses made.

You know the old saying: "Beauty is only skin deep, but ugly's to the bone. Beauty dies and fades away, but ugly holds its own!"

Challenges a woman's thinking, doesn't it? It's rather intimidating and frustrating for us females. We are going to get old in spite of face-lifts. If the face is lifted, what about the skin on the hands and neck? One cannot be having cosmetic surgery constantly. Besides, the mileage is recorded on the inside, no matter how many lifts are done. Am I being abrasive? I hope not, women.

True, lasting beauty is of the spirit. If one can be "ugly to the bone" that has to mean we possess an ugly spirit. A sweet-spirited old woman is beautiful, but a mean-spirited one is a sad scene, indeed. I have looked at the pictures of Corrie ten Boom from the time she was a young girl until she reached the late eighties. Corrie has grown more beautiful with each passing decade.

Therefore, doesn't it behoove us "Eves" to get right on the inside and cultivate that inner beauty through faith in the God who created us and the love expressed for us by His Son, Jesus Christ?

The Source of Sparkle

Like most women my age, I have occasional and (sometimes) persistent aches and pains. At the present, I am suffering with my right shoulder and leg. There are days when I feel quite young, and those are the days when I tend to overdo. Some mornings my muscles remind me that time is getting on and that I am on the homestretch of three score and ten.

I praise God for bringing me, by His amazing grace, thus far. And His grace will take me home when it is time. *Grace.* What a beautiful word! What does it mean to you?

Is grace a lily springing tall from the ground? A swan gliding across a clear pond? An eagle, dipping and soaring across a cloudless sky? Every one of these images of beauty is God-given. However, the greatest meaning of the word *grace* is "unmerited favor." What a gift. The grace of God is the gift of His Son Jesus Christ to redeem us and mold us into His fashion.

Women, this is "where it is at." The greatest friend and benefactor of woman is Jesus Christ. He can take an ugly duckling and transform her into a beautiful swan. He can work this miracle with us women, no matter how we look. We may be dumb, smart, tall, short, slim, or fat, but ". . . the flesh profits nothing; the words that

I have spoken to you are spirit and are life" (John 6:63).

When He quickens the spirit of woman with her permission, she starts to sparkle. Given full sway in her life, He can and will polish her into a very precious and beautiful gem for His crown.

As for me, I simply want to do the will of God in my life. The Lord knows that I'm no saint—far from it—but because of the Holy Spirit Jesus promised, I am being sanctified day by day, bit by bit, from image to image.

Some days I don't feel sanctified at all! I hurt in my very bones; my eyesight isn't always the greatest. Other times I am very tired and weak, and then it is difficult to feel gloriously triumphant. However, within the recesses of my soul that wellspring of joy bubbles, independent of my human feelings. We cannot depend on feeling, we must depend upon the Word of God. We must know that He cares, that He is watching over each one of us all the time. The well-known cliché, "This, too, will pass," is right on in terms of stress on mind, body, and spirit.

Stress is a part of life and sometimes I think the Lord gives me some double doses just to remind me about His peace. For instance, one night recently I was in the airport in Green Bay, Wisconsin, enroute to Escanaba, Michigan, for a Salvation Army program at the armory. Since on several traveling occasions my bag has not caught up with me, I travel with "luggage wheels," upon which I stack my loaded garment bag and carry-on case with enough "threads" to see me through the engagement. Well, I guess I'm not the only person who has the same idea. Another woman deplaned in Green Bay, grabbed my garment bag (identical to hers), and simply disappeared. I had no idea this had happened, and merrily took what I thought was my clothes hanger into the women's room to rearrange my things. As I zipped it open, I nearly fainted, for there was absolutely nothing familiar in it, For a minute, I thought I was in an Alfred Hitchcock movie.

Grabbing the bag, I ran all the way through the airport to the entrance, in an effort to exchange it for my own. To my dismay, the woman had left. However, dangling from her bag was a tag bearing her name and telephone number. I thanked the Lord for His providence in small details. The lost-and-found department called the number, but there was no answer. They finally reached her ten minutes before I was to depart for Escanaba.

What could I do? I left the woman's clothes hanger at the lost-and-found department and departed for Michigan, with nothing to sleep in but my panty hose and blouse. I know when you're on stage, it doesn't pay to look rumpled. It took quite a bit of grace to maintain Christian equanimity, but I survived without exploding. The wardrobe hanger arrived at 11:00 A.M. the following day, just in time for a change of clothes for rehearsal and a long dress for the night appearance.

Yes, it takes a lot of grace in such situations. And it takes God's grace to laugh at yourself when you know your "juniors" are laughing at, as well as *with* you. It takes grace to be smilingly serene, when you hear strangers say, "How old *is* she?" "Is that really Dale Evans Rogers?" "She looks younger than she does on television." (Or, "She looks *older*.") "She's heavier than she used to be," or, "Does she really believe all she says

about Christianity?" "Where is her cowgirl outfit?"
"Why is she traveling alone? You'd think she would at
least have a secretary with her!" "Why doesn't she
check her luggage, instead of pulling that thing on
wheels through the airport?" "Is that her real hair or a
wig?" "Do you think she really wrote those books or
had a ghostwriter?"

To the latter question, I want to reply, "Yes, I have a
ghost writer—the Holy Ghost."

It takes grace, when a young gas attendant or a
stewardess calls you "Madam." Those are the times I
have to remind myself of the many miles I have come
with the Lord, of the blessings He has showered upon
me and mine, of the great family we have, of His faith-
fulness in being with me.

The glorious fact is that I am still on my feet! There are
times when I feel younger than springtime, and others
when I feel as old as Methuselah. Some mornings,
when I have had my necessary quota of sleep, and be-
hold the bright sun streaming across the desert, the
birds chirping in the trees in our backyard, I don't feel
any older than when I was a child. The wonder and joy
of simply being alive floods my being. Then I look in the
mirror, and the face gazing at me strangely resembles
the face of my mother, when she was my age. *Mother,
did you have this experience as you grew older?*

What's important? It's how we feel on the inside, not
how we look on the outside. The Bible says that man
looks on the outward appearance but God looks on the
heart (1 Samuel 16:7). The real person is inside, and the
beauty of that inner person is what will count, when
everything is over and that inside person takes flight
from this vale of tears.

I am constantly hearing women say, "These wrinkles have simply got to go!" Or, "I'm going to have them smoothed out by a face-lift." Women, those outside wrinkles will keep coming back from time to time. But what about those inside wrinkles of the spirit: *frustration, resentment, bitterness, jealousy*. A good shower of the Holy Spirit does wonders in smoothing lines of dissatisfaction and petulance. I have seen some incredibly smooth, shining faces in old women who have never heard of a face-lift. Invariably, they have been the faces of giving, happy-spirited women, who are more interested in the welfare of others than in themselves. These women have that unconscious grace and beauty that shines from within.

Full to the Brim

One of the nicest things which happened to me recently occurred when one of my grandchildren, watching me bustle about in the kitchen, said, "Grandma, why aren't you old?" *Well,* I thought, *you can go on asking questions like that forever!* Then she added: "You really don't seem old, grandma. I thought all grandmas were old, but you have a good time!" The illogic of children!

Yes, I do have a good time, because I'm happy inside—happier than at any time of my life. The term "full of years" certainly applies to me, but being "full of faith" transcends it. Why should I want to look as I did in my twenties? I wasn't happy in my twenties. In a newspaper article, an internationally famous photographer was asked if he had actually refused to photograph a world-famous superstar. "Yes," he replied. "All I saw in her face was love of self, and that's boring." He lamented the influence of standardization upon the mass media, and said:

> I wish the youth today would search to express individuality, to find what they like, rather than follow others, and I wish the not-so-young would feel that maturity is beautiful and refuse to worship youth or run to a plastic surgeon with their first character lines, which can become their stamp of charm and individuality. How much more beautiful Eleanor Roosevelt was in her later years, when her irregular features were bathed in the beauty of her giving nature.

Please don't get me wrong. I am delighted if someone compliments me by saying I am youthful. For I believe:

> Yet those who wait for the LORD
> Will gain new strength;
> They will mount up with wings like eagles,
> They will run and not get tired,
> They will walk and not become weary.
>
> Isaiah 40:31

Woman, the eternal *you* springs from the eternal *Spirit!*

11
Woman, Where Are You Going?

Women get so busy *doing* that sometimes they don't stop to contemplate *where* they're going. There's so much to do. We run from one task to another, complaining about too little time to accomplish everything.

Life is a race, with a course and a destination, not a treadmill going nowhere. How do we get off the treadmill and onto the track?

For years I raced without any idea of where I was going. I knew where I wanted to be, as a wife, a mother, and a career woman, but I was not always very calm about the direction I was going.

Sometimes it seems easier just to sit and let the world swirl around us. Don't get involved. Let someone else do it. Be content.

I don't believe that life needs to be a whirlpool, carrying you in circles, or a swamp, covered with weeds where your boat is stuck. Life is an adventure, if you are following the right Guide.

We have to answer the question, "Where am I going?" in our own way. The details of our day-to-day activities are determined by the importance each of us places on our journey.

My best ideas come to me early in the morning. If only I could arouse myself to write the thoughts that come tumbling into my sleepy head. Inspiration is so elusive. It slips through your fingers and out of sight quickly. So many times when traveling in my car on the way to the L. A. Airport, insights flood my mind, and I'm unable to write them. I always promise myself that I will remember to jot them down at the first stop. However, I have been down the road for a pretty "fer" piece, my eyes have seen much, and it's not easy to recapture that sudden burst of inspiration.

Right now I'm having a cup of instant coffee in my motel room in Bremerton, Washington, across from Seattle. Outside my window there is a picture of incredible beauty. This is certainly God's country. Now I realize that there are many places of magnificent scenery in America, so I hope I'm not going to offend all of you patriots outside the State of Washington. But let me tell you about this scene.

The motel is situated on a lagoon, an inlet on the peninsula. The water mirrors a clear, blue sky, fringed with fir trees. There are bevies of ducks swimming leisurely within view of my window. A sailboat rests on the opposite shore. (Do you want to join me now?) Flanking my porch is a stately fir tree, arms gracefully extended upward and outward. I now know why the Lord has given me this quiet moment. I must close my eyes to all of this beauty to think only of Him.

Lord, let me, as a Christian woman, be a living tree for You.

I have noticed on the plants in my home that a new shoot always reaches upward first, and then outward. This is the function of a Christian—*upward* toward God and *outward* toward man. Isn't this a picture of the Cross of Christ?

Please, God, don't let me be a Christian isolationist, content to perch atop a high hill in an ivory tower, waiting for the Rapture. Let me be where the action is, where the need is, where the hurt is—for that is what You did on earth and You expect the same from those who call themselves by Your Name.

Dreams and Desires

Once in a while, when I'm being interviewed, I'm asked if there is an unfulfilled dream in my life, what are my desires and hopes? I believe that dreams are important in life. When we stop dreaming and hoping, the light and excitement leave us.

Psalms 37:4 says, "Delight yourself in the Lord; And He will give you the desires of your heart." If I delight myself in Him, He will place the right desires within me—desires that will fulfill my potential for which He created me—desires that will glorify Him and ultimately make me happy.

For a time I wanted to do a dramatic role in a Christian film, or a secular film which would be helpful in a spiritual or philosophical way. It didn't happen. I realized that this ambition was my own desire to do a part like this, and instead of manipulating or maneuvering, I should commit it to the Lord. By His grace I was able to turn it over to Him and relax in the knowledge that His will be done.

At this point in my life, I value every day as a precious gift; my greatest desire is to be pliable in God's hand, to be used of Him as He chooses. Therein lies the way of peace for me.

As I travel around the country, I see the people whose dreams and desires are poured into the lives of others, and of the joy they have in touching others. Let me tell you about my visit with the wonderful volunteer force at the Baylor Medical Center in Dallas. I addressed these men and women on the twenty-fifth anniversary of the facility. What a spiritual lift it was to congratulate those people for their selfless service in this beautiful hospital of some twelve hundred patients. I could see the humble appreciation on their faces as they received the awards, but their real joy, as many said, was "in the doing." Our Lord said it is more blessed to give than to receive, and how true those beautifully wise words of our Savior are. While on earth, He was the living example of giving one's self, never asking in return. When He told us to love our enemies, He knew it would be hard, but He also knew it would bless us and ultimately make our enemies be at peace with us. However, women, unless we take the time to go apart and let God minister His Holy Spirit to our inner person, loving and giving is almost impossible.

There Is a Law

When I think about the direction of my life, and the urgency for all women to know where they're going, I can't help thinking about the greater picture of the direction of America. If we have the privilege of being an American, and if we have even a grain of sense about us, we certainly must be concerned about what is happening in our great land today. America is hurting, and its pain is being felt in every sector. It's hurting us in our families, our economics, our quality of life. It seems when things go wrong, someone pops up with the cliché "There oughta be a law!"

I agree. There "oughta be" a return to *spiritual* Law. There was a time when God's standards were sought in our country .The first schools of learning were Christian, and the precepts taught were in the Judeo-Christian tradition. Today there are many who say we can survive without spiritual Law. This is like saying we can jump off a building and go up! I'd like to point a finger at some nebulous mass, like the government, and say, "It's your fault that we're in this mess." But that's not true. It's all *our* fault. We have been quiet, when we should have been talking. We have been tending to our own business, when we should have been noticing those who were trying to take away our business! We can do so much, however, as women, for the return to basics: *love of God, respect for authority, high moral standards*.

It is incredible to me that one atheistic woman could bring about the elimination of prayer in our schools. America was founded by men and women of prayer, supporting each other and training their children in the way they should go. I've often wondered what kind of childhood Madalyn Murray O'Hair could have had to motivate her in her personal crusade to abolish God

from our educational system. Did she have a mother
who really cared about the development of her as a
whole person—mentally, physically, and spiritually?
What a power a woman of Mrs. O'Hair's determination
could exert for turning this country toward the real
Source of her greatness!

Modern-day Deborahs

Concerned women today are wondering what they
can do to halt the disintegration of moral standards in
America. Should we be at the forefront of the battle or
behind the lines? I believe we have to be both places—in
the forefront by speaking out and standing up for God's
principles; in the background by undergirding our husbands and teaching our children. This is no time for
idleness or monkey business as usual.

Perhaps from the ranks of Christian women we will
see an increase in modern-day Deborahs. Do you know
her story? It's an inspiring account of a woman in Israel
whose faith in God strengthened an entire nation.

Deborah lived during the time of the Judges, centuries before the birth of Christ. She was an obscure
woman, and yet she changed the course of the nation of
Israel. For years Israel had lived under the oppression of
an alien king. Times were really bad. Many people had
turned to the worship of idols, forgetting the Lord God
of Israel and His guidance. Deborah was known
throughout the land for her ability to counsel people.
She would sit under a palm tree, and people would
come to her with their problems; she would give advice.
(If she lived in our time she would probably have an

office someplace with a nameplate saying FAMILY COUN-
SELOR on the door.)

But this woman, Deborah, was more than a counselor. She was a gifted woman, who cared about her
country and was indignant over the lack of leadership
among the men of Israel.

Her country was in trouble, and this homemaker believed that God would come to the rescue of her
people—if they would honor Him. She rallied one of
Israel's strongest generals to the cause of gaining victory
over the enemy. She was even able to convince this
military man that the Lord would deliver the enemy
into his hands. Can't you just see it? Here was a
woman, talking to the commander-in-chief of the com-
bined forces, and saying, "Look, Barak, if you take ten
thousand men and march up to Mount Tabor, I promise
you that the general of the enemy forces will surrender
to you."

Listen to what the brave, intrepid leader of the nation
of Israel said to this little woman: "Okay, Debby, I'll go,
if you will go with me. But if you won't go, it's no deal."

Deborah trusted God implicitly. She said, "I'll go
with you, but I want you to know that the victory will
be the Lord's not mine."

And God did destroy the enemy of Israel, the king of
Canaan, just as Deborah had prophesied.

If you read the fifth chapter of the Book of Judges you
will find a song which this "Mother of Israel" sang. It's
a tingling song of patriotism, giving all the credit to God
for the victory! It was the "Battle Hymn of the Republic"
of its time.

Sometimes I want to join in that song. In fact, there is

a line that says, ". . . And you who travel on the road—sing!" (Judges 5:10). Yes, that's what I do. I sing when I travel on the road—sing to the glory of the Lord God who can save America from its enemies—if only we would trust Him and believe in His power.

It sends shivers through me to think of what would happen, if women all over America would rally against the enemies of our land, ". . . against the rulers, against the powers, against the world forces of this darkness, against the spiritual forces of wickedness . . ." (Ephesians 6:12).

How strong we can be, women, when we have God working through us! All we need to do is to be alive in His Spirit. The Song of Deborah could be a rallying cry for our generation, for every one of us:

Awake, awake, Deborah:
Awake, awake, sing a song! . . .

Judges 5:12

Where are we going? To a state of being alive, to awaken America to the need—to return to the Lord God of Israel and to His Son.

Where I'm Going

I do not have to see all the way to the end of my sojourn on earth. God gives me enough light to see where I am, and I'm not afraid of where I'm going. I can depend on His company for the rest of my life. He's a great traveling Companion—the best!

In Nashville, some time ago I recorded these words in Marijohn Wilkin's song "Where I'm Going":

Sometimes it seems like I'm standing still
Until I look back and see how deep my valley
How high the hill
And each step nearer to eternity.

Sometimes my friends misunderstand
'Cause I hear the sound of a different drummer
But I know my life is in His hands
Just as sure as autumn follows summer.

I know not what my future holds,
Lord, I have no way of knowing.
But I know the One Who holds my future,
And I have no fear of where I'm going.

As one approaches the autumn and winter of life, a very growing concern emerges. *Has my life helped any other struggling human being? Have I been concerned mostly with self?*

Jesus said, ". . . whoever loses his life for My sake . . . shall save it" (Mark 8:35). I have found this to be absolutely true.

Am I afraid of the future? Not on your life! "For God hath not given us the spirit of fear; but of power and of love, and of a sound mind" (2 Timothy 1:7 KJV).

I shall go forth in the power of His Holy Spirit, being assured of a sound mind through Christ Jesus.

In Jesus Christ, I can become truly WOMAN!